Turn Your Passion
Into Profits

Turn Your Passion Into Profits

BY Janet Allon

AND THE EDITORS OF Victoria MAGAZINE

HEARST BOOKS

New York

Library of Congress Cataloging-in-Publication Data
TURN YOUR PASSION INTO PROFITS: HOW TO START A BUSINESS OF YOUR DREAMS.
p. cm.
Includes bibliographical references.
ISBN 1-58816-006-8
1. New business enterprises—Management. 2. Small business—Management.
3. Home-based businesses—Management. 4. Self-employed.

HD62.5 .T87 2001
658'.041—dc21   00-058078

PHOTOGRAPHED ON THE FRONT JACKET: top right, Paula Goldstein (left) of Desana; bottom left, Michéle Rosier of Flowers by Michéle
FRONT JACKET PHOTOGRAPHS: upper left, Jim Hedrich; all others, Toshi Otsuki
BACK JACKET PHOTOGRAPHS: upper left, Michael Skott; upper and lower right, Toshi Otsuki; lower left, Andreas Von Einsiedel

First Edition
1 2 3 4 5 6 7 8 9 10

DESIGNER • ALEXANDRA MALDONADO

Printed in the United States of America
www.victoriamag.com

Acknowledgments

I would like to thank all of the entrepreneurs and business owners who gave generously of their time and wisdom via e-mail, phone, fax, and face to face. Also, thanks to Jane Applegate, the small-business champion and guru, and CEO of SBTV.com; Clifford Ennico, small-business attorney and host of the *Money Hunt* on PBS; Lisa Linden, CEO of Linden, Alschuler & Kaplan, a public relations firm in New York City; and accountant Steve DelSanto, of DelSanto and DeFreitas, CPAs in Closter, New Jersey. Finally, thanks to my husband, Tom Allon, for his support and ever-instructive small-business war stories.

—Janet Allon

Table of Contents

Foreword

The greatest happiness is to transform one's feelings into actions.

—Madame de Staël (1766-1817)

I am convinced that tucked in the depths of every woman's mind is an inventive, long-simmering idea for a business. In the last twenty-five years, so many women have opened their own entrepreneurial doors that the number nearly equals that of male business ownership. Impressive.

Since its inception in 1987, *Victoria* Magazine has encouraged women's efforts by featuring their shops, clothing, designs, furnishings, flowers and restaurants and, in turn, has often been credited with giving those businesses an all-important first boost. We continue to share news of women's creative endeavors on our pages—which is why it is no surprise that *Victoria* is the number one magazine read by women who are self-employed as well as the number one magazine read by women who are the owner or partner in a business.

Turn Your Passions Into Profits affirms *Victoria's* commitment to all of you budding entrepreneurs by telling you exactly what you need to know at the onset of a venture. It includes invaluable comments from women who have experienced successful start-ups to help you avoid pitfalls and establish a strong framework for success.

If I had this book when I actually had a product it might have encouraged a real business. Making my own necklaces led to numerous compliments and a serious order from a high-profile Fifth Avenue store. Elated at their request for my first dozen pieces (it never occurred to me that orders would come only by the dozen!), I knotted the papier-mâché pearls with pastel silk cord and sewed snap-together satin ribbon bows late into many nights. It took me three weeks to finish, meticulously pack, and proudly hand deliver them! When the necklaces sold out, I got another order—this time for three dozen; they had to be ready in a month. Clearly, with a full-time job, I couldn't cope and managed to talk my mother into producing them for me, with the caveat that I would supply all the elements and handle delivery. We encountered a quality-control issue with my bead source, found a dyer so we could provide a bronze finish and threw up our hands in defeat at the next order.

I wasn't prepared, had no plan, no backup, no sense of pricing, and thank goodness, did not really have to make a go of it, as I loved my magazine editor's job. In retrospect, I may have missed a major entrepreneurial opportunity. Armed with this book and the wisdom it provides, I would have known exactly what to do. Herein you'll have a map to follow, which can turn your dreams into a fulfilling reality.

Peggy Kennedy
Editor-in-Chief
Victoria Magazine

Introduction

I do not know anyone who has got to the top without hard work. That is the recipe. It will not always get you to the top, but should get you pretty near.

—Margaret Thatcher, English prime minister

The secret is out. Women have and always have had what it take to start, run and grow businesses. Attributes like creativity, resourcefulness, courage, persistence, an instinct for what people want, optimism, and the ability to work long and hard and learn from mistakes are hardly the exclusive domain of men. And when a woman combines a passion for what she's doing with a business venture, she can be as unstoppable as a force of nature.

Women-owned small businesses are creating a quiet revolution in this country and beyond. From the small, one-woman freelance service businesses to multimillion-dollar, name-brand conglomerates like Martha Stewart, Donna Karan, The Body Shop, The Thymes Limited, and many more, women are coming into their own as business owners and transforming the economic landscape.

For every large-scale, well-known success story, there are hundreds of littler ones—women carving out very satisfying existences making money while doing what they love. You don't have to grow a huge company to succeed, be profitable, and experience immense satisfaction. Ambition and success come in all sizes.

The numbers show that when it comes to entrepreneurship, women have indeed come a long way, and in a relatively short time. As recently as 1973, women owned just 4.6 percent of the businesses in the United States.

By 1996, that number had jumped to 35 percent, and by 2000, women had nearly evened the field with their male counterparts. Between 1987 and 2000, the number of women-owned ventures in this country doubled, from 4.5 million to 9.1 million.

This entrepreneurial activity on the part of women shows no sign of abating, and it is not only affecting the lives of the women business owners themselves, but those of hundreds of thousands of people who work for them. As employment at large corporations declines, it is growing at women-owned enterprises, which now employ more people than the Fortune 500 combined.

Women are proving equally adept at running businesses geared toward male and female consumers, but one reason that women are starting more and more businesses, no doubt, is the realization that women are a potent consumer force. In the United States alone, women account for some 80 percent of consumer spending. Who better than women themselves to recognize what it is that women need and want, and to provide these services and products as perhaps no one else can? Examples abound. Successful shoe designer Vanessa Noel designs fabulous-looking women's shoes that are also comfortable, a facet of shoe design that male designers may have overlooked. Camilla Bergeron, who sells antique and estate jewelry, brings her discerning feminine eye—what she calls a "woman's touch"—to the once male-dominated jewelry business. Her idea is deceptively simple: Jewelry should look attractive on a woman, not just be loaded with precious stones and metals. "What gets people coming back," she says, "is wearing jewelry they get compliments on."

The experience of running a household or raising children has spurred some women entrepreneurs to recognize and capitalize on some need they realized other women must share. That was the case for Gail Smith-Peterson, who started her successful children's clothing line and store—Buckingham Mercantile—with no formal design or business experience, when she had trouble finding clothes big and cute enough for her larger-than-average baby boy. The numbers support the notion that women bring their own brand of ingenuity to the workplace. Statistically, women are less likely to inherit family businesses than men, but they are more likely to start a business that solves some problem or void faced by women in the marketplace.

As more and more women prove they have what it takes to run businesses, financing for these businesses is becoming more accessible. When it came to securing lines of credit and financing, women have historically faced certain very real obstacles. Fortunately, these barriers are gradually being removed, at least legally. In 1988, Congress passed the Women's Business Ownership Act, aimed at ending discrimination in credit to women entrepreneurs. Commercial banks have grown more open to lending women-owned companies money. More work still needs to be done to help women gain access to venture capital, but women are starting to network and share ideas about how to get their share of these funds.

Still, though the legal obstacles no longer exist, many women are reluctant to seek outside financing for new business ventures, preferring to rely on personal savings, family money, and credit cards. Other women lack the courage of their convictions or the confidence to strike out and create a business of their own.

To all those who harbor a secret entrepreneurial desire, but hesitate because of lack of experience or confidence, the overwhelming advice from entrepreneurs who have taken the plunge is *Go for it!* Take the chance of loving what you do every day, of experiencing the pride of ownership, and reaping the rewards of your own labor. But you have to go for it all the way, heart and soul. The faint of heart need not apply. And before you begin, arm yourself with information, research, plans and ample self-knowledge.

In the pages that follow, you will get a valuable introduction to starting your own business. You will be guided—step by step—through the process: From coming up with and honing a business idea, through planning and financing a start-up business, to staffing it and keeping track of the all-important numbers. You will gain insight into the differences between wholesale, retail, mail order and web-based businesses; learn what it takes to start a service business; and become more savvy about marketing, advertising and publicity. Though not a workbook, this book will give you concrete pointers on how to draw up contracts, calculate start-up costs, and figure out your profits and losses. It will tell you what to ask and what not to when hiring someone. The book ends with a discussion of how to evaluate whether it is time to expand and grow beyond your start-up idea.

Interspersed throughout are the inspiring—often amusing—stories from women entrepreneurs who are already living what you dream about. Their pluck, can-do attitude, and willingness to speak frankly about the challenges and exhilaration of being a business owner are immeasurably useful. Their voices and frontline experiences are wonderful and instructive to read. Think of them as some of your first mentors.

Through it all you will get a realistic sense of what it really takes to turn your passion into profits and embark on a career as an entrepreneur. It is not the road to travel if you are looking for the easy way, but, if personal fulfillment in your work is a top priority, few things compete with venturing out and starting, creating, and building a business that is a true expression of you.

It's them as take advantage that get advantage i' this world.

—George Eliot, English writer

There is only one success—to be able to spend your life in your own way.

—Christopher Morley,
Where the Blue Begins

Before You Begin

Being an entrepreneur isn't something I'm trying to do. I am creating and doing the things I enjoy, while using my passion to build the business from and around them. Creating a business around my passion is natural to me. My ideas fuel my energy and drive my ambition. I am constantly creating at my business and at home. I don't know how not to!

—Gail Smith-Peterson, Buckingham Mercantile,
Cardiff by the Sea, California

Why Go into Business for Yourself?

Starting your own business is exciting, exhilarating, creative, and not a little terrifying. Few of life's experiences offer the thrill and variety of a new business venture. It takes both courage and conviction. As an entrepreneur, you are putting your vision and yourself on the line in a way that is vastly different from working for someone else.

What makes entrepreneurship compelling to increasing numbers of women? When you own your own business, there's no such thing as a "glass ceiling." Your earning and growth potential are less limited. Your experiences and work life will likely be more varied than with a regular job on someone else's payroll.

Many women who start their own business are attracted to the independence, flexibility, and freedom to follow their own instincts and take their own risks that owning their own business affords. When you are your own boss, although you are bound to work hard, you also have much more control over your hours and the role your work plays in your life. As Pamela Scurry, the owner of Wicker Garden and Wicker Garden Baby in Manhattan, says, if eating dinner with your family every night is an all-important goal, you can arrange your professional life to meet that goal— and still be very successful.

Some entrepreneurs just have problems working for other people. They have more confidence in their own judgment than in that of others, and bristle at authority. They have reached a point in their life where they want to be the beneficiary of their own hard work, which is understandable. Entrepreneurship can become a way of life. "My theory is that entrepreneurs are unemployable," laughs Margaret Jones, co-owner with her sister of Scriptura, a fine-paper emporium in New Orleans.

Some women entrepreneurs fall into their businesses as inevitably as rain in the tropics. Creating or collecting something beautiful comes as naturally to them as breathing, and leads inexorably to selling it. Their whole life points them in the direction they need to go. Some simply followed a lifelong passion that seemed to blossom naturally into a business of their own.

SUCCESS STORIES

❖ PAT KERR designed clothes for herself as a teenager and traveled the world collecting antique lace, ceremonial robes, and scarves. Her business designing wedding gowns and other special-occasion attire became a near overnight success when she made an appointment and took some of her collections and designs to Neiman Marcus, sold everything, and was commissioned to design several Neiman Marcus windows. Now her multifaceted company offers baby couture, bridal couture, and even produces enormous events like inaugurations. "I feel lucky to have become what I was meant to be," she says.

❖ GAIL PITTMAN began designing and making plates and decorative pottery at her kitchen table when her children were small and she was at home caring for them. At the time, she was just fulfilling a craving for a creative outlet, with no idea that she stood at the threshold of a hugely successful business. Each time she had a show, her lovely handpainted creations sold so well, she was able to expand her business. By the time her children were older, she had a thriving enterprise that continues to grow twenty years later.

❖ CLAIRE MURRAY moved to Nantucket from New York City to raise her daughter and live a quieter life running a small inn. Soon she became enthralled with the colonial craft of rug hooking, and began designing and making her own rugs inspired by her beautiful surroundings. On the off-season, she hosted "learning vacations" at her inn, where travelers could learn to hook rugs themselves. She bought the local yarn store to ensure her supply of wool. These days Claire Murray has become a formidable name in the design of all kinds of housewares, from the floor to the kitchen cupboards, bed linens, and more. The company has twelve retail stores, numerous licensing agreements, and thriving catalogue and web-site sales.

What all three of these women discovered, was that they not only had talent as designers, they also had previously undiscovered talents in business. Maybe you do too.

Business as Self-Expression

Perhaps more than any other kind of money-making activity, owning your own business gives you greater opportunity to express yourself, and, many say, this results in a deeper feeling of satisfaction and fulfillment with your work. "Owning and running a business," says the designer Claire Murray, "is creative in and of itself." There are other benefits as well. The journey itself, regardless of the degree of success attained, makes many women more creative and confident in their own abilities, qualities that enhance the rest of their lives and even those of their children. Clothing designer Isabel Garreton puts it eloquently:

> I found in having my own business a sort of territory that has allowed a projection of my persona that I did not anticipate. It has expanded my physical world through travel, my exchanges with people, my comfort with assertiveness, and my acceptance of the cut-and-dried components of what works and what doesn't. It has translated into an appreciation of life and opportunities that I believe has benefited my three daughters and their perception of strength.

BUT... THERE ARE ALWAYS BUTS...

Starting a business, entrepreneurs emphasize, is far from easy and the farthest thing from romantic. Women entrepreneurs have to laugh when they hear about someone who wants to start her own business because she envisions being able to take it easy, work shorter hours, and enjoy longer lunches with friends. Joyce Ames, a veteran entrepreneur who handcrafts exquisite fabric-covered lampshades, puts it bluntly. "The advantage of owning your own business is that you can't get fired."

Owning your own business requires more knowledge, time, planning, resources and energy than working for someone else. One rule of thumb, say experts, is to estimate the amount of time you think you'll spend on your business, then double it. The payoff, say entrepreneurs running businesses that stem from their true passions in life, is that the time spent is among the most satisfying in their lives. The pride of ownership is exceeded possibly only by that of raising a good and happy child. And so, though work—and a lot of it—is very much part of the entrepreneurial equation, it somehow seems less grueling than other work. It is truly a labor of love, and the potential rewards, go way beyond profits. Though profits are nice too.

As Debby DuBay, owner of Limoges Antiques in Andover, Massachusetts, puts it: "Your business will be successful because it is you. You thrive because of the gratification that success and your accomplishments bring. Now, that does not mean that it is not a lot of work. On the contrary, it just means that you are fulfilled, happy and content when you fall into bed from exhaustion."

THE PERSON

We all have a little bit of the entrepreneur in us. But some people show an enterprising spirit even early in childhood, going beyond the usual lemonade stands and Girl Scout cookie sales. Here is the story June Matheson, who has started several antiques and home furnishings stores in Vancouver, tells to illustrate her early entrepreneurial flair:

> We had an amazing apple tree in our backyard; I think the species was Kings. They were like large grapefruits. I was eight or nine and could see how much my school buddies coveted these wonderful fruits. For some reason, I didn't feel any shame about selling apples to my friends. I sold them for a nickel, and on the way home I'd head for the local bakery and buy as many donuts as I could with my day's take. I went on to sell Christmas cards door to door. I sold lots because in those days, not too many people were into personalized cards, and that's what I pushed.

Entrepreneurial skill is a curious combination of traits and smarts and desire—it's the ability to see and seize an opportunity where others might not, coupled with the yearning to run your own show. It is certainly not the same as having earned good grades in school or possessing advanced degrees. In fact, many of the world's most successful businesspeople—male and female—have been far from A students. The entrepreneurial urge and inspiration can be fed by the everyday lives women lead.

Successful entrepreneurs tend to have a determination, passion, and a positive attitude that helps carry them through the toughest times. They have the heartfelt conviction that their product/service is the best and that they are just the person to offer it. They are willing to take what to some may seem like a risk but to them feels more like a very good bet. And they like to win. Here's what Helen Cox, founder of the As You Like It Silver Shop in New Orleans, says about her early life:

Looking back on my life, I can see how elements of an entrepreneurial personality developed. As a young teen, I was an AAU swimmer and liked to win. I went to a large public high school where I was vice president of the senior class and voted "most likely to succeed." In college I was vice president of the student body. I majored in psychology and took several business courses. Being hired by Sears for their management-training program was a wonderful part of my life. We were sent to the sales floor, accounting department, shipping docks, personnel department, etc., for various lengths of time. I learned every aspect of retail business from a master.

WHAT THE PSYCHOLOGISTS SAY

Some of the traits that psychologists say are found in many entrepreneurs include persistence to the point of stubbornness, a strong personal need for success, a certain rebelliousness against authority, an ability to learn from mistakes, an overall optimism and willingness to see problems as challenges to overcome, a willingness to make short-term sacrifices for long-term gains, a desire to be in control, an enjoyment of being alone, curiosity, flexibility, and a certain visionary and experimental approach to things.

But just because you don't think you possess all of these traits does not mean you shouldn't start your own business. It may mean you will need to find a way around some of your weaknesses, perhaps get a partner who complements them. The important thing is recognizing your strengths and your weaknesses so you can develop strategies to either capitalize on or overcome them.

Is Entrepreneurship for You?

SOME QUESTIONS TO ASK YOURSELF

(Adapted from the Small Business Administration's Women's Online Business Center)

1. Are you a self-starter? There won't be any boss breathing down your neck when you own your own business. It'll be all up to you to initiate projects, make deals, clean up messes...

2. Do you get along with different personalities? When you own your own business, you need to work with a wide variety of people: vendors, servicepeople, customers, staff, the press, bankers, etc.

3. Are you good at making decisions? You will face decisions every day as a business owner. Can you make them quickly and independently?

4. Do you have the physical and emotional stamina? Owning your own business often requires twelve-hour days, and six- or seven-day workweeks. The going may get tough both physically and emotionally.

5. Are you good at planning and organizing? Many business failures could have been prevented by better planning and organization.

3. Are you extremely motivated to succeed? Many successful entrepreneurs say that the possibility of failure never entered their mind. They exhibit incredible tenacity. The road to success is often bumpy. True entrepreneurs try and try and try again.

7. How will it affect your family? The demands of your business may well compete at times with the demands of your family.

INNER AND OUTER

Being an entrepreneur is a curious combination of inner and outer. It means finding the place where your passion and the needs of the marketplace meet. First, you need to discover or tap into your deepest dreams, loves, and desires. Only something you are passionate about will carry you through the inevitably tough times involved in running your own business. If you are not doing something you love, you will become discouraged all too easily, and succumb to the temptation to give up before you have given your all. Pamela Scurry, owner of Wicker Garden and Wicker Garden Baby in New York City, is passionate about antique wicker, as well as heirloom-quality baby furnishings and clothes. Sylvia Varney of Fredericksburg Herb Farm is passionate about herbs. Paulette Knight grew up in a family of sewers, studied textile arts, and became an expert on and importer of French wired ribbons well before she sensed a void in the retail marketplace and opened her successful notions shop, The Ribbonerie, in San Francisco.

But here's the catch: It is not quite enough to fulfill your own dreams and fantasies. And not every hobby or interest can be turned into a successful business. You also need to find the people who will share them. That is,

> *An entrepreneur is someone who has a lot of drive and no trust fund.*
>
> —Margaret Jones, Scriptura, fine-paper emporium in New Orleans

there has to be some need to tap into for what you are selling. And if the need does not quite exist, then you have to ferret it out and help create it. In some cases, like Paulette Knight's and Sylvia Varney's, and countless others, you'll face the not-unpleasurable task of educating your consumers about your wonderful product.

Chances are that if there is something you genuinely enjoy offering, there are people out there who would love to receive it. The trick is finding those people. That, in a nutshell, is marketing. More on that, later.

ASSESSING YOUR SKILLS

You may have skills that would be useful in starting and running a business that you have never thought of in this way. Keeping a household on a budget, planning for a trip, shopping for a family of four, for example, all demand organizational skills that are helpful in running a business. Having an eye for bargains or color, having good instincts about people, having good communication skills—like being able to write a good letter—are all strengths you may be able to draw on. In your professional life you may have discovered and cultivated talents you can draw on in the service of your own business. Perhaps you know graphic design, are a good negotiator, or are a born saleswoman.

In fact, as an entrepreneur, you will find yourself drawing on your previous life experiences in ways you never suspected. Before opening Limoges Antiques in Andover, Massachusetts, Debby DuBay was serving her country as one of the first group of women recruited into the Air Force in the 1970s. She says the lessons she learned in the military carried over into her life as an entrepreneur.

> My basic philosophy as a Commander was to set my men and women up for success. I did that by emphasizing training, education, research, experience, and mentorship. I also encouraged my troops to understand their own personality including their weaknesses and strengths, and to understand their personal goals and desires. So, when I decided to start my own business, I decided to use my own advice.

Setting yourself up for success through thorough research and profound self-knowledge is a great way to start. Not to mention a great way to live.

Remember, many skills, especially business skills, are learnable. If you lack some skill that you think would be necessary for running a business, chances are there is a course, web site, book (like this one) where you can

Tapping into Your Skills

Some Questions to Ask Yourself

- What are your main strengths?

- What are your more serious weaknesses?

- How would someone else answer those two questions?

- What are your talents?

- How much do you know about the business, industry, or field you are considering?

- What business skills do you possess? (sales, accounting, negotiating)

- What entrepreneurial skills do you have? (initiative, risk-taking, self-confidence, and the ability to learn from mistakes)

learn it. Skills that aren't learnable are often hireable. You don't have to be good at sales to hire an expert salesperson, although certainly, any owner of a small business is, to some degree, in sales. You don't have to be good with numbers to hire an accountant. What is most important is that you understand your own limitations.

On the other hand, just because you have never done something before does not mean you won't be good at it. Many entrepreneurs recommend a very hands-on approach to all aspects of the business, especially when you are starting up. The education is invaluable, and you may discover skills and aptitudes you never dreamed you had.

INSPIRATION

Entrepreneurs get ideas for businesses from just about every aspect of life. Some get them from hobbies, others from some recollected childhood passion. Cookie Washington learned sewing from her mother and grandmother, made clothes for her Barbie doll, and today custom designs wedding gowns and soft accessories, including her unique and lovely "kiss bag."

Have you ever had a thought that begins something like, Why isn't there a store for… , a service that caters to… , or the like? If a need occurs to you, chances are others are experiencing it. Voids that you perceive in the consumer landscape may be the seed of an idea for a business.

Some get their ideas from entering a new stage in life, such as motherhood, and discovering a niche or a need, as Gail Smith Petersen did when she had trouble buying cute, durable clothes for her much larger-than-average baby boy. Some savvy businesswomen start businesses to fill a need that they as consumers have not been able to fill elsewhere. Necessity is truly the mother of some of these innovative businesses. Jacquelynn Ives had been a teacher in New York when her husband was transferred to Wisconsin and she found that her teaching credentials were not transferable. She had to do something to make a living, and so she tapped into a childhood love of china patterns and table settings, and ended up starting Jacquelynn's China Matching Service. What had once seemed like one of life's setbacks turned out to be a great stroke of luck. Her business has flourished for more than a quarter of a century.

> *A successful business pulls you toward it.*
>
> —Paul Hawken, *Growing a Business*

Then there are those creative souls who find themselves starting down a path of setting up their own business without realizing this was where they were headed. New Yorker Wells Jenkins was an architect who made herself a necklace of charms based on a dream she had one night. When she started receiving compliments from complete strangers about the necklace, suddenly it clicked for her that she might design and manufacture deeply personal and unique jewelry using clients' photos and keepsakes.

Carol Bolton knew she liked scouring flea markets, and had a knack for putting objects together in an appealing way. Fortunately, her husband enjoyed the same thing. Their business started just by buying and reselling things that they had bought and loved. Now the couple own five stores in Fredericksburg, Texas, and Carol has launched a related career designing and licensing antique-looking furniture.

Christine Dimmick always liked to cook, and as a hobby cooked up fragrant beauty potions in her kitchen after a full day at her job. When she brought some of her potions to work, her co-workers started ordering so many that she eventually gave up her day job in order to start The Good Home Company based in New York.

Other women have first had the general idea that they'd like to start a business, then done some research to figure out what sort of a business might work. Kate Flax, founder of Kate's Paperie, with four stores in New York City, knew she wanted to open a store and tried to figure out what store-crammed New York City needed. Her idea for fine-paper stores coincided with both a need in the marketplace and a personal passion.

Sylvia and Bill Varney moved to Fredericksburg, Texas, from Houston because they were looking for a slower pace of life. Once in Fredericksburg, they got the entrepreneurial itch and tried to figure out what the local retail landscape was lacking. Eventually they opened a store that sold name-brand herbal bath products. When they discovered they preferred growing and brewing their own herbs and potions, their business grew into a multifaceted enterprise with gardens, recipes, a multitude of herbal products, a spa, books and a web site.

RESEARCH

You will have to do a great deal of research in order to maximize your chances for success. You need to be the expert in your particular field, whether it is 18th-century linens, aromatic herbs, designing the perfect wedding dress for slightly overweight women, fine silver, antique ribbons, designing gardens for urban dwellings, or whatever. If you are genuinely passionate about the item or service you are selling, then this research will not seem like a chore, but rather like a labor of love. Many entrepreneurs particularly enjoy the educational aspects of their business and sharing their knowledge with their customers.

Passion is a good start, but it won't carry you all the way through. You need to do your homework. Research the competition, the field, the costs. Who else is doing what you do? How can you do it better? You will need to research locations and suppliers.

Finally, you will need to research the mechanics of owning and starting a business. This book is one resource, and will share many others with you. In addition, find out if there are low-cost courses offered in your area to fill in some of the gaps in your knowledge.

MENTORSHIP

Many entrepreneurs who are just starting out fail to take advantage of a resource that is both precious and free—the advice of other, more seasoned businessmen and businesswomen in their industry. Seek out veterans and business people who are well-enough established so they won't be threatened by you. Consult with organizations of women entrepreneurs to find people who can advise you. The Small Business Administration has counselors who are formerly successful retirees who are happy and flattered to offer their advice and hard-won wisdom through a program called SCORE. No one understands running and growing a business like another entrepreneur, preferably one in a similar industry.

"If you can, find a mentor within your industry," suggests Mary Ella

Gabler, whose twenty-seven-year-old business, Peacock Alley, is a premier supplier of bed and bath luxury items. "I learned everything from scratch, and it takes much more time."

Debby DuBay, of Limoges Antiques, sought the advice and assistance of business professors, retirees, and local businesspeople and CEOs before opening her shop. In addition to gleaning some advice and wisdom for herself, she found that she was also doing them a favor. "Most people love to talk about themselves and are flattered when you ask them for advice or assistance," she says.

Finding a Niche

It really is not enough to say, "I want to open a dessert business, or a jewelry business, or a cosmetics business." You and every other entrepreneur need to find a niche. When the jeweler Camilla Bergeron started her New York-based business, she brought her expertise as an investment banker to the task. Although she knew she wanted to sell jewelry, she also knew that the world did not exactly need another antique and estate jeweler. She had to find a way to separate herself from the pack. "You need to have a point of view," she says. "I thought I had something to say." In fact, Bergeron has enough to say that she does not just sell jewelry, she lectures on it. And in her day-to-day business, her point of view on jewelry means that sometimes she steers customers away from items that are inappropriate for them, even at the risk of losing a sale. "I don't want people wearing something that does not suit them or is tacky," she says.

Karen Krasne, who started Extraordinary Desserts in San Diego twelve years ago, says that people come up to her all the time saying they too want to start a dessert shop. Her advice to them: "Find a niche." In her case, finding a niche meant starting small, working in a restaurant where she was responsible for desserts, getting feedback from the customers, and finding out if what she liked to make—exquisitely tasty and pretty French desserts—was marketable on a larger scale. When she finally opened her dessert and coffee shop, there was no such thing as just a desserts shop. Needless to say, the landscape has changed with the advent of Starbucks and others, and Krasne needs to constantly change and evolve to set herself apart, offer more, and, as she says, keep her customers "stunned."

If you intend to start a business selling something that you make yourself, something beautiful and unique, then part of your niche is built in, since presumably no one else is making and selling precisely the same artistic creation you are. But you still need to find out if there is a market for your designs, products, or service. Finding a market and a niche is not an exact science; even seasoned designers find themselves sometimes designing and making things that just don't sell. But lampshade designer and maker Joyce Ames believes that true craftsmanship never goes out of style. "There is always a need for beautiful, high-quality handmade things," she says.

Market Research

Finding a niche leads you directly into market research. Market research is something that you may be doing in an informal way without even being aware that you are doing it. It starts when you ask, Where can I get... ? Why isn't there are store for... ?, or when you start polling your friends and acquaintances to see if they also would welcome the chance to buy the service or product you envision. When they can't get that product or service, where do they go?

More formally, market research is a term for figuring out who your customers are, whether there are enough of them to make your business really viable, and who your competition is. It is an incredibly important part of planning, starting, and running a business. In your preliminary research, you need to read trade journals for your area of interest, join trade groups, read relevant newspapers and magazines, and talk to potential supplies and customers. The information gained in doing market research is also part of a well-constructed business plan, which will be discussed in Chapter Three. But even before you start down the road to starting a business, when it is just in the concept stage, you can do some market research by assembling a focus group of friends and potential customers to discuss your product or service and find out what they would be inclined to buy.

Market research does not end once the business starts. Far from it. It is an ongoing process vital to keeping a business healthy and growing. Successful entrepreneurs urge people who want to start businesses to listen carefully to their customers and their needs, which is an ongoing form of market research. Karen Krasne, who owns Extraordinary Desserts in San Diego, originally offered nothing but exquisite French desserts and coffee all day long. When enough of her customers asked for muffins in the morning, she realized she had to adjust her vision to accommodate them.

MARKET RESEARCH HAS TWO PARTS:

1. Identifying the competition. What is out there already? What stores, catalogues, web sites, etc., offer something similar to what you would offer? The reason for identifying the competition is so that you can set yourself apart from it. If you can't improve upon what already exists in terms of quality and/or service, you might want to rethink your game plan.

2. Identifying your customer. For example, "My customer is typically a thirty-five- to fifty-year-old female, owns her home, works full or part-time, has an income of between $30,000 and $50,000.

Through these processes, you can figure out where the opportunities lie in the marketplace.

Sometimes, market research will help you realize that there is no real need for the type of business you envision. While disappointing, that's an important realization. You will have to rethink either your product, service, or location.

STUMBLING ON A NICHE

Some businesses have sprouted from a simple act of generosity: making a present for a friend.

❖ PEACOCK ALLEY, a twenty-seven-year-old purveyor of luxury bed and bath linens, started out with a modest pillow given to friends as a Christmas present, says owner Mary Ella Gabler. "People liked it so much, we decided to make more, and sold a collection to Neiman Marcus."

❖ STONEHOUSE FARM GOODS AND TRACY PORTER, a design business, sprouted when former model Tracy Anne Porter presented a hand-painted tray to a friend at her bridal shower. When opened, the present inspired such a chorus of "oohs" and "ahs" and requests for more, that Tracy figured she must be on to something, borrowed money to attend the New York Gift Show with samples, where she and her husband, John, received $74,000 worth of orders, and their business was born.

❖ KEVIN SIMON always harbored dreams of being a designer, but it was not until the clothes she designed and made for her entire family drew so many compliments and inquiries on the streets of Buffalo, New York, that she figured those dreams could come true. She took her whole family west with her to the more hospitable climate of Venice, California, to open her clothing boutique.

❖ KAREN SKELTON took a pottery course just for fun and to escape the corporate world she inhabited as a graphic artist in New York City. When a friend invited her to take some of her pots to the New York Gift Show, Karen received about 7,000 orders. At that point, she realized she had no choice but to build a studio and go into business for herself.

If you are lucky enough to be clever with your hands and make beautiful things, such creativity is probably its own reward. But consider the possibility that it could be even more than that. If you find that the things you make are subject to the admiration of strangers and friends alike, you may have found yourself a potential business.

SOME QUESTIONS TO HELP YOU HONE IN ON A NICHE

- What need does my product or service fill?
- What is my competition?
- What advantage does my business hold over the competition?
- Can I offer higher-quality service?
- Can I create demand for my product or service?

As you answer these questions, you begin to see the possibilities of spinning your passion into a business, straw into gold.

Decisions, Decisions, Decisions

You gain strength, courage and confidence by every experience in which you really stop to look fear in the face.

—Eleanor Roosevelt

Long before opening day, you will face myriad decisions about your business. You may as well get used to it. Owning a business, being your own boss—and possibly the boss of others—is in part about making decisions every day. From whether to sell your wares from a shop, a catalogue, or via the web to whom you hire and when to give raises, where to advertise, or whether to open a second location, the choices will come fast and furious, and demand that you make them.

The desire to make your own decisions, to be master of your own ship, is in fact what drives many people to be entrepreneurs. There will be large and small decisions, fundamental forks in the road, and tiny choices in details. Will your business be a service business, like catering or gardening or interior design? Or will you produce a product for sale? Perhaps you will be a dealer of some sort; someone who buys things, like antiques, and resells them for a profit. For this type of business, you will need to make frequent decisions about what and how much to buy. Will you work at home or rent a space? Will you take a partner or fly solo? Will you start small and part-time and keep your day job or dive all the way in? It all comes down to what you want.

Although decision-making can be lonely, you do not have to make all of these important decisions alone. You can begin your networking early. Find the relevant trade association, professional groups, and seek out mentors to help you even in the initial concept stage. Consider seeking out entrepreneurs you admire and asking how they started.

Timing Your Busines

NOW OR LATER?

When is the right time to start a business? The decision is not unlike the decision of when to start a family. Each is a huge life-changing commitment that is likely to consume a significant part of your energy and time at least for the first couple of years. But since so many factors must come together in order for a business to launch, some would say seize the opportunity whenever you can.

Timing is a personal decision; there is no one right answer for everyone about when it is best to start. There might, however, be some collected wisdom about when *not* to start a business. It might be wise to postpone a launch in the wake of energy-draining or upsetting life events, the loss of someone very dear, a move to a new area, or the birth of a baby. Since you may be unable to draw a salary from a fledgling business for the first six months or so, launching at a time when you have some savings to fall back on, or another way of paying your bills, is recommended by many.

But for every bit of advice, there is an example of someone who started a successful business at a time when conventional wisdom would have urged more caution. Pamela Scurry was seven months pregnant when she opened her first Wicker Garden store in New York City. Tracy Anne and John Porter were newly married and had just moved from Chicago to rural Wisconsin when their first business, Stonehouse Farm Goods, sprang to life. Necessity is so often the mother of invention in business as well. Many a successful enterprise has been launched by a woman right after divorce or loss of another job, precisely when her back was up against the wall.

Sometimes timing is a matter of recognizing and seizing an opportunity in the marketplace—and the ability to do so is the hallmark of many entrepreneurs. You cannot afford to be too rigid in your ideas about when is the right time to do things. Opportunity does not always present itself on a precise schedule.

A lot of success stories hinge significantly on a sense of timing, of being ahead of an oncoming wave. Leslie Ross, the founder and creator of The Thymes Limited, started brewing her soaps and fragrances well ahead of the boom in high-end beauty products, a boom she may well have helped create. Karen Krasne's Extraordinary Desserts in San Diego, where desserts and fine coffee are served all day, presaged Starbucks and survived the onslaught of coffee bars by consistently staying ahead and offering something slightly different. As a businessperson, the last thing you want to do is play catch-up—you want to set the pace and let others try and catch you. Of course, you don't want to be so far ahead that no one understands what you are doing, including your potential customers. Luck is an element of good timing—luck and extraordinary instinct. If someone is already doing what you propose to do, then why do it unless you can do it a whole lot better, a whole lot more cheaply, or up the ante in some other way?

PART-TIME OR FULL-TIME: THE VIRTUE OF THE GRADUAL START

Some savvy entrepreneurs test the waters before they jump all the way into a new business. Christine Dimmick brewed her fragrant natural bath and home potions at home after work and offered them to her co-workers. It was only when she received an overwhelming volume of orders that she realized she might be onto something big, and finally relinquished her day-time job to start the Good Home Company at the ripe old age of twenty-five.

Karen Krasne also went about starting her dessert business cautiously for the first few years. After training in France, she became the dessert chef at a small upscale restaurant where she was able to get lots of feedback on her creations. It helped her define her style and gave her some self-esteem. At the same time, she was doing research on the marketability of her product, and doing it, as she says, "on somebody else's dime." Her next step was to take her wares around to restaurants and bakeries, selling them whole-sale. "I wanted to find out if people appreciated what I was doing," she says. Only after success with clients like Neiman Marcus did she finally have the confidence to open her own retail establishment in San Diego twelve years ago, Extraordinary Desserts.

If your business idea lends itself to a slow and gradual start that will enable you to test and research your market, gain confidence, tweak your product, make a little money on the side, and keep your income and benefits coming, the gradual start is worth considering. But at some point, like Dimmick and Krasne, you'll have to decide whether or not to take the leap. Then, there's no looking back.

Service or Product?

Make no mistake, service is an important part of any business, and customers gravitate to businesses where great service accompanies quality products. Amazon.com upped the ante in terms of customer service in the book-selling business. White Flower Farm raised the stakes in the garden catalogue industry. But neither of these two successful companies is fundamentally a service business.

In a true service business, your customers become clients, people with whom you have an ongoing relationship, and your product is *you*: your labor, your expertise, your vision, your time, and your creativity. Your involvement with your clients is much more intense, and the job is only complete if they are satisfied. You need to be able to sense their desires, tease them out in conversations, anticipate them, and quench them. Some of your clients will be easy, some will be tough and demanding, but regardless, you'll still have to deal with their myriad personalities. If this degree of ongoing people-reading and people-pleasing is not for you, you might want to rethink starting a service business. When you are offering a product for sale (either one you make yourself or one you buy and sell), you still need customers to like what you do enough to spend money on it, but ultimately, they are buying a thing, not renting you.

Of the approximately eight million women-owned businesses in the United States, more than half, or 52 percent, are service businesses. The service industry is booming, economists say, and many see the sector as ever more ripe for growth. Busy Americans need services as never before and are increasingly willing to pay for services they once performed themselves. More people have more disposable income and less time. Plus, good old-fashioned service never goes out of style. It has, however, become harder and harder to find, and opportunities have sprung up for those who can spot them.

In general, service businesses, (especially home-based service businesses) have lower overhead and lower start-up costs. Relationships, creativity, and contacts require no storage space, and you don't need to lay out any money for inventory. The exception is if you are opening an inn or a restaurant, both of which are service businesses, and can be very costly. But your decision to start a service business cannot be based on economics alone. Self-knowledge is essential.

"I like making people really happy," says Charmaine Jones, whose Hoboken, New Jersey-based company, Isn't That Special Outrageous Cakes, does just that. Jones's cakes for weddings and other special occasions are extremely detailed and whimsical artistic creations. But the desire to create "as little problem for the client as possible" is part of what makes it a success as a service business.

We will delve into the fundamentals of starting a service business in more detail in Chapter Six (page 102).

The other kinds of businesses are manufacturing, retail, and wholesale. A manufacturing business, where you make something, generally needs to be combined with a way of selling that thing, either retail or wholesale, and sometimes both.

Retail or Wholesale?

Retail and wholesale are not necessarily mutually exclusive. Many businesses manage to combine both very successfully. These days the choices have grown more complicated. You can have a mail-order or Internet retail or wholesale business as well. But when you are starting out, you generally need to consider one or the other. You might develop a strategy of opening a store for a specific amount of time in order to get exposure for yourself and your product, and eventually sell via the web, mail-order, or even wholesale. When you have a store, your livelihood depends on people finding you, which is why location is so important. When you have a wholesale business, you have the option of seeking out your customers, either through trade shows or by making appointments with buyers from stores you think would be interested in selling your product. Your decision of whether to sell wholesale or retail may also be dictated by the type of product you plan to sell.

Like so many aspects of starting your business, the decision of whether to sell retail or wholesale needs to be made with ample self-knowledge. The important thing is that the style of your business is a good match with your personal style, so that you can pour your energies into being successful at your chosen business.

Does a lot of contact with people keep you energized and happy? Or are you more of a solitary sort, who would prefer to pour your energies into dreaming up designs or thinking at a computer? Storeowners have to deal with the public on a daily basis, stay on their feet and do a lot of chatting with sometimes uninformed customers.

Are you friendly, approachable, and service-oriented? Do you mind doing a little hand-holding with your customers when they are not sure what they want or need? Do you mind being tethered to a store? It is not for everyone. Joyce Ames, who designs and makes lampshades covered with vintage fabrics, says she knew early on that retail was not for her. "My father forbid me from going into retail," she says. "He said I didn't have the temperament for it, that I'm too impatient. He was right."

Just about anyone can acquire the basic social skills of being a shop owner, but if such sociability and patience goes against your nature, you may want to consider another way of getting your goods to the public. You'll still need to get out there and sell or hire someone to do it for you. But, as Ames says, "You'll have more maneuverability. You can go out and seek your clients."

Chapter Five will go into greater detail about the various selling strategies, retail, wholesale, mail-order, and web site, to help you decide which ones are right for you.

What's in a Name?

Names create impressions and are often the first thing your customers know about you. It can help to have an accessible and memorable name. Many businesses are simply named for their founder and creator. It both personalizes the business and suggests that it is a reflection and an expression of a particular person—you. Many designers name their businesses after themselves: Isabel Garreton, Charlotte Moss, Cynthia Rowley, Claire Murray, Tracy Porter, to name just a few. Everything they make has their signature, their name, their brand, their style. When that name becomes well known enough, people begin to know exactly what they can expect from a product bearing that name. The companies are as individual as the founder. The name is elastic. It can stretch and grow with you. Unless you are very sure that you only want to make or sell one thing, it's better not to limit yourself. What happens when Jane Brown's Scarves decides to branch out into hats?

The disadvantage of naming a business after yourself is that people will not at first know what it is you are selling. Not until you become better known. Another approach is to choose a name that tells prospective customers exactly what you are selling. Anyone who comes across the name Limoges Antiques, Debby DuBay's shop in Andover, Massachusetts, can be pretty certain that Limoges china is sold there. Similarly, garden designer Rebecca Cole originally named her Manhattan-based business Potted Gardens, making it plain that gardens and plants in containers were likely to be found there.

Still others take a more whimsical approach to naming, and who is to say they are wrong? Even apparently nonsensical words can become part of the popular lexicon if the product is good enough. Look at Gymboree and Häagen-Dazs. Some choose suggestive ancient, foreign, or foreign-sounding words: Kate's Paperie, Scriptura, The Ribbonerie, Archivia Books. For her store and line of children's clothing, Gail Smith Peterson invented a mascot worthy of a children's storybook, a moose named Buckingham, and named the store Buckingham Mercantile, inspired by old-time general stores. Whispering Pines, a mail-order business offering "things for the cabin," was named after the area where the founders spent their youthful summer vacations. They hoped the name would be as evocative for customers as it was for them. It is also possible to go the route of choosing a name that is appealingly fanciful. Jenny Feldman named her Harbor Springs, Michigan, store Pooter Olooms Antiques, in part because she liked the sound and in part because she wanted to leave herself the possibility of selling a wide variety of merchandise.

The common thread in naming your business is that the name should have some meaning to your business and link to your overall philosophy and the mission of your business. You should be able to explain why you named your business as you did, since people will certainly ask you and your employees about it, if the meaning is not immediately clear.

From a legal point of view, the only restrictions on business names are that the name be available in your state, meaning no one else has registered a business under that name, and that the name not be deceptive or misleading. A name that is too similar to that of another business may create some confusion, however, and loss of potential customers.

TIPS ON NAMING

- Research the competition. What kinds of names catch you? Which are hard to remember?

- Bounce your name ideas off friends and strangers.

- Make the name easy to understand, say, spell, and remember.

- Make sure the name you choose for your company is connected in some way to its overall mission and philosophy, in a way that both you and your future employees can explain.

- Make a list of several names you like when you go to register yours, in case some are taken.

- As soon as you have selected a name, look into whether you can reserve it as a web domain as well. Even if you are not going to put up a site immediately, it costs very little to hold a web domain name.

Choosing a Legal Structure for Your Business

Whatever kind of business structure you decide to set up, you'll need to consult with a trusted lawyer and/or accountant who can help inform you of the legal and tax implications of each. But don't leave such an important decision in the hands of so-called experts, no matter how much you trust them. And do your research before consulting with professionals who charge high hourly rates. As with many aspects of entrepreneurship, tap other business-people for advice about structuring your company. Their war stories can be extremely instructive about both the pitfalls and benefits of each. Learn from their mistakes. Get your information from a variety of sources. You need to have a firm grasp on the facts and implications yourself in order to make a well-informed decision.

There are three basic choices for structuring a business:

SOLE PROPRIETORSHIP

This is just you operating your business, either under your own name or under a trade name like Janine's Graphics. Legally you and your business are one and the same. The sole proprietorship is by far the most common type of business, probably because it is relatively uncomplicated and inexpensive and people can set them up without hiring a lawyer. You do still have to register your business with your local county clerk's office. Usually there is a fee of not more than $125. The Small Business Administration estimates that there are approximately 15.3 million such business in the United States.

Advantages: The sole proprietorship is the easiest type of business to form (and to dissolve) and affords you the greatest flexibility. You have all the control, make all the decisions, and receive all the profits. Also, you can write off business expenses on your personal income tax form.

Disadvantages: Chief among the disadvantages of sole proprietorship is the fact that this structure affords you and your family's assets no protection. If you encounter financial problems or are sued, your personal assets are at risk. If you take out a loan and the business fails, you are personally liable for the loan. You can get some insurance to protect yourself from certain kinds of lawsuits, but you are still liable for everything related to the business. It behooves you to educate yourself about what kinds of insurance you need, since ours is a litigious society. Also, it is generally harder to raise capital and to attract high-quality employees with a sole proprietorship.

PARTNERSHIP

You can have one or more partners who are co-owners of your business. As with sole proprietorships, legally there is no distinction between the company and its owners. Also, each partner is fully liable for the actions of the other. It is vital to draw up a legally binding partnership agreement stating how decisions will be made, profits shared, disputes resolved, partners added, partners bought out, or the partnership dissolved. Like a prenuptial agreement, it may seem cynical to figure out how things will be divided in the event of a "breakup," but such an agreement is vital. Partnerships do break up, and at a higher rate than marriages. Without a partnership agreement, all partners are assumed to hold the same share of the company.

Advantages: Partnership makes entrepreneurship a little less lonely; it means having someone to bounce ideas off, someone to help in the decision-making, an extra pair of eyes and hands. Like a sole proprietorship, partnerships are relatively easy to form and afford a fair amount of flexibility. All partners have a say in decisions, and partnerships incur a minimum of government control and paperwork. There is a tax advantage of passing income and losses directly to the partners. It can be easier to raise money for a partnership business than for a sole proprietorship.

Disadvantages Each partner is fully liable for the actions of the other partners. You have to share not only the decision-making but the profits. The equity of each partner is not liquid and is at greater risk. It's harder to sell a partnership interest in a business to an outsider. If one partner dies, the firm has to be liquidated, unless legal safeguards are in place allowing the business to continue. The family of the deceased partner is entitled to the assets of the partner.

An advantage or disadvantage, depending on your perspective, is that any partner can dissolve a partnership without permission from, or even consultation with, the other.

There are various kinds of partnerships: limited, nominal, silent, and secret. Despite the relative simplicity, it is inadvisable to form any kind of partnership without using a lawyer to formalize the arrangement.

Partnership Wisdom from Entrepreneurs

It is a very rare person who has all of the traits needed to conceive of and run a successful business.

—Sylvia Varney, Fredericksburg Herb Farm

Partnership is like a marriage or worse. Don't look for someone you get along with. Look for someone you can fight with and get over it.

—Jane Goodrich, Saturn Press Cards

Partners make the good times more fun, the hard times more bearable. Partners are people to talk, debate, noodle and argue with. People to grow with.

—Paul Hawken, Smith & Hawken, in *Growing a Business*

Even if your partner is someone in your family or someone you're intimately involved with, like a boyfriend, make it official. Have something in writing about what percentage each person gets, whether they're 30 percent owner or whatever. That way, if they are working hard, they know exactly what it is for. And include something about buy-out potential. Keep an open door.

—Karen Krasne, Extraordinary Desserts

Find someone whose skills are complementary to yours. That way you won't want to be doing the same thing all the time. Discover a mechanism to get through fights—because you are going to have fights. Keep your sense of humor.

—Cynthia Conigliaro, Archivia Books

Once the business is established and it's a success, don't take in a partner when you can hire an employee.

—Joyce Ames, Joyce Ames Lampshades

Choosing a partner is the hardest thing in the world. It's better to have someone who has strengths that you don't have. Once you're in a partnership, it's not all sweetness and light. Sometimes you go to bed mad. You just have to try not to let disputes go on for too long.

—Camilla Bergeron, Camilla Dietz Bergeron Antique Jewerly

CORPORATIONS

In general, this business structure is a legal entity separate from its owners, who are shareholders. The owners do not necessarily run the business day to day. The shareholders elect a board of directors to oversee the major decisions and policies. To incorporate, contact your state agency that handles incorporation and request the form to incorporate—and use a lawyer. Filing fees and legal fees generally fall in the range of $1,000 to $1,500.

Advantages: The chief advantage of the corporation is the limited financial liability of the owner(s). Personal assets are not attached to the corporation and are not at risk. Also, unlike a partnership or sole proprietorship, in the event that one of the principals dies, the corporation continues to exist until it is legally dissolved. Corporations can raise funds by selling stock. The corporate structure is an extremely well-defined and established relationship between shareholders, officers, and employees. It can work for businesses that are large and small, profit and nonprofit.

Disadvantages: Corporations are more complicated and expensive to form, requiring a Certificate of Incorporation to be filed with the appropriate state agency. There is more government control here, and more that must be reported. You'll have to fill out corporate tax returns or pay an accountant to do it. Depending on the state in which you incorporate, you may also have to pay annual state fees.

Just because you incorporate does not mean you are a huge company. There are several types of corporate structures. The smaller variety is referred to as a Subchapter S Corporation, which allows no more than 75 shareholders. With S corporations, taxation is also simpler, with the same advantages as a sole proprietorship or partnership, while maintaining the limited liability of the corporation. With C Corporations, taxation is more complicated: Corporate earnings are taxable before earnings are distributed to owners, who are again taxed on whatever is distributed to them.

Yet another option is a LLC, or a Limited Liability Company. This business entity is less complex legally than a corporation, shares the tax structure of a partnership, and offers the limited liability of a corporation.

What kind of company should you form? There is no one right answer or perfect structure, and you will want to consult a lawyer and an accountant before making a final decision. "Generally," says Cliff Ennico, small-business attorney, "the less you are concerned with limiting your liability, the less legal complexity and hassle you will be forced to deal with."

Work at Home or Get a Space?

Home is not just where the heart is, it may also be where the money is. According to *Money* magazine, some 13 million Americans own and run home-based businesses, 25 million if you count part-timers and moonlighters. Full-time home-based entrepreneurs earn an average of $58,000 a year after taxes.

For mothers who want to be home with young children yet still earn a living and pursue a career, working at home can be both a flexible and inexpensive solution. If you are starting a business on a shoestring, a home-based business offers much lower overhead. Working at home is not an option for every type of business, but advances in technology, including computers, e-mail, web sites, and telephone voice-mail, have enhanced people's ability to conduct business easily and professionally from home.

You can always start your business at home and make the decision to move out and rent a space once it takes hold and expands. It can be a daunting but necessary transition, as Gail Pittman found out. "When you move your business out of your house, all of a sudden, you have overhead. You have other people depending on you," she says. "It can be quite overwhelming, and you need to be prepared for that increase."

ADVANTAGES OF WORKING AT HOME

Financial: Your overhead is substantially lower and you have the benefit of writing off a portion of your home expenses on your taxes.

Flexibility: Your hours may be just as long as or longer than a job outside of the house, but you can structure and have more control over your time.

DISADVANTAGES OF WORKING AT HOME

Separation: Separating your work life from your personal life becomes tricky. You may end up working all the time. Your family also has to adjust to the fact that although you are at home, you are not always available. This is especially difficult for young children.

Professionalism: Working at home requires more self-discipline—it's very easy to procrastinate by doing chores or puttering. If your business is one where you need to see clients, the at-home business can seem less professional to them.

Isolation: Some women find working at home to be lonelier than they anticipated, especially those who have just left a job outside of the home. When home and work are in one spot, there is the danger that you will find yourself getting out a lot less often.

Audits: The IRS is slightly more likely to audit small, home-based businesses.

If you do decide to operate your business from your home, you need to look into any zoning restriction that might apply and your state's laws regarding work certificates or licenses. Call your local zoning board, community development office, or planning department for information on what kinds of home-based businesses are disallowed. Like any other business, a home-based one needs to be registered with the county clerk and to have a sales tax number. In addition, it is wise to be as unobtrusive to your residential neighbors as possible. Keep work-related noise, traffic, and odors at an absolute minimum.

TIPS ON WORKING AT HOME

- If at all possible, set up a separate room or area of your home just for business. This will help you keep your business and personal lives separate and allow for the home-business tax deduction.

- Get an insurance policy to cover your equipment and inventory. Ask your broker about an in-home business policy. If you are seeing clients in your home, you need a home office rider in case they hurt themselves while in your place of business.

- Whenever possible and if appropriate, arrange to see clients and customers outside of your house, at a local restaurant. It might not be wise to invite strangers into your home.

- Keep detailed records (especially in case of an audit). Daily appointment books are good for jotting down daily expenses as well as meetings with clients.

- Keep separate bank accounts for business and personal uses.

- Set up a dedicated phone line just for business. Consider getting voice-mail; it makes your operation sound bigger and more professional.

- Consider getting a mailbox for your business at Mail Boxes Etc. or other such storefront service. This is better than a post office box because it has a street address. These commercial mail centers also take deliveries, mail packages, and help you keep yourself organized.

- Expect to spend from $3,600 to $8,500 for basic business equipment, including a computer with modem, a fax machine, and a laser-quality printer.

Here's what Gail Pittman, who started her dinnerware and table accessory business at home when her kids were small, advises about running a home-based business: "Have a good work ethic and be professional about managing your time. Set boundaries. Decide when home life begins and don't take business calls or make appointments during that time. A separate phone line with voice-mail is a must. Also, remember that if you were working outside the house, an eight-hour day is all you would be required to work."

Choosing a Location

For some kinds of businesses, like owning a store, working at home is not an option. The choice of location should come only after thorough research, since a poorly chosen location can present serious obstacles to success. Some businesses make the mistaken assumption that success in one location guarantees success in another, then learn a hard and expensive lesson on the importance of the right location.

Helen Cox, the owner of As You Like It Silver Shop on Magazine Street in New Orleans, found this out when she opened a second store in Laguna Beach, California, on the Pacific Coast Highway. She reasoned that a lot of Orange County customers shopped at her New Orleans store while on vacation, but found they were less interested in shopping in a branch of her store near their home. She also had problems with theft and break-ins. "One of the mistakes we made," says Cox, "was not thoroughly researching the property out there. We later discovered that we were in the wrong location and we closed that store after a year."

Location plays a different role depending on the type of business. For a retail store that depends on walk-in customers, its location is said to be everything. Madison Avenue in New York, Newbury Street in Boston, and Magazine Street in New Orleans, for example, reliably attract hordes of well-heeled shoppers looking to part with their cash. Picturesque tourist towns like Fredericksburg, Texas, and Andover, Massachusetts, also have built-in appeal. Of course, you'll pay a premium for the most desirable real estate and will have to sell a lot more product to meet that high overhead. The location you choose also relates to your pricing structure and the kinds of customers you hope to attract.

If your business really takes off, it becomes a destination in and of itself. L.L. Bean has not been hampered by being in tiny Freeport, Maine. White Flower Farm may be hard to find, but customers—lots of them—manage to find it. A successful business may even help to transform an area. Pamela Scurry opened her Wicker Garden shop on a part of upper Madison Avenue that shopkeepers had not dared to consider commercially viable before that. She chose it because it was all she could afford at the time. Before too long, other upscale shops followed her example, and the whole area became increasingly attractive to wealthy customers. The lesson? "If you become a destination," says Scurry, "people will come."

With a wholesale manufacturing business, location still plays a role, but there are other factors to consider than just making sure customers can stumble on you. Karen Skelton set up her Potluck Studios, a wholesale pottery business and store, in Accord, New York, a picturesque village about two hours north of New York City. Rents were cheap, but the Catskills town still attracted some tourists, and Skelton is close enough to make the all-important annual sojourn to the New York Gift Show.

Sometimes, location will play an unexpected role in your business. Gail Pittman happened to live in the college town of Oxford, Mississippi, when she started making ceramic dinnerware, showing it, and selling it. College students bought her wares and took it to their homes all over the country, giving her nationwide exposure that contributed to the growth of her business.

Sometimes the place itself becomes the inspiration for the business. Sylvia Varney says that it was the town of Fredericksburg, Texas, that fired her and husband Bill's entrepreneurial imaginations. It's a prosperous town that attracts tourists and boasts horse racing, pecans, peaches, and a place in the history of World War II. "We wanted to contribute," says Sylvia.

Claire Murray did not move to Nantucket, Massachusetts, from New York City with the intention of starting an international business. She was just looking for a healthy place to raise her daughter. But Nantucket became and remains the inspiration for many of her rug designs, a small business that has in turn spawned a retail, wholesale, and licensing empire.

THINGS TO RESEARCH WHEN CHOOSING A LOCATION

- Proximity to potential customers
- Where the competition is located
- Accessibility to potential employees
- Convenience for you
- Near public transportation, parking
- Overall business climate in the area
- Market rents in the area
- Any zoning or signage restrictions
- Safety of the area
- Proximity to suppliers
- Nearby amenities like restaurants and banks

LOCATION STORIES

Gail Smith Peterson wanted to expand and relocate her children's clothing and decorative accessories store, Buckingham Mercantile. Here, she explains her process of finding a new spot.

> After deciding to relocate my Mercantile, I began by listing where and why I wanted to move. I did a little survey with my customers on the locations where they enjoy shopping. It was just out of my own curiosity and to set up focus areas to canvas for the new location to fit my needs and criteria.
>
> HERE ARE SOME OF THE ITEMS ON MY LIST:
> Visibility, street appeal • Large windows for display • Square footage Neighboring tenants • Price, terms of lease, etc. • Charm, unique and potential Tenant and customer parking • Not in a mall or shopping center.

It still took Peterson nearly two years of driving around daily to find the perfect spot in Cardiff by the Sea, California.

Where you locate your business may also depend on where you have chosen to live. Jane Goodrich, a greeting-card maker and the owner of Saturn Press, and her husband had already decided to live on a remote island in Maine, because the land prices were affordable and because they planned to renovate a historic house there from scratch. The business came as a secondary way to make money. Here's what Goodrich says about her location:

> The location is both a handicap and a help. It is a handicap because of all the inherent shipping problems given our island location. There is an employment problem as well in a place like this with few people, and it is difficult to find educated, motivated employees.
>
> On the other hand, there is a tremendous romance factor to our island location that seizes people and helps them remember both us and our products. We welcome visitors, and it is remarkable how many find their way to our doorstep. Once they visit, they never, never forget us.
>
> As a business, we rather welcome the isolation, and we count our remoteness as a plus. We are already as big as we want to be, and we find that not listing our phone number is an advantage, since telephone time is often unproductive. Not only that, but we are a greeting-card company, and want to encourage people to write. It has certainly worked out that the people who go the extra mile to find us are usually our best customers, partly because they are the type of people who "go the extra mile," and also because they enjoy ferreting out small and exciting companies to produce products for their customers. If you are everywhere, you are not unique.

Writing Your Business Plan

Looking back on our business plan, I am amazed at how many of the dreams we had have turned into reality. I would encourage all entrepreneurs to have a plan in writing and try to stick to it.

—Margaret Jones, Scriptura

CHAPTER THREE

The Importance of Planning

If you decided to take a trip to a faraway place, you might not necessarily know how to get there. To increase your chances of arriving at your destination and minimize the chances of getting lost, you would likely do some research and get directions and a map. You might take note of some milestones along the way to mark your progress and make sure you are on course. Just as you would not set out on a journey to a new place without a map and some planning, you should not embark on a business without a plan. A business plan is your map, your compass, and your route all wrapped in one.

Planning is essentially a process in which we set goals and identify our ways of reaching them. Planning a business is all about setting measurable and realistic goals or targets and figuring out the steps we need to take to hit them. While it is disappointing to set goals and not reach them, it is downright treacherous not to set goals at all. Here's what Margaret Jones, the co-owner Scriptura, fine-paper and stationers in New Orleans, says about writing a business plan:

> We spent a great deal of time writing a business plan. During that time, we were forced to crystallize our business objectives and project incremental growth stages of our company. Looking back on our business plan, I am amazed at how many of the dreams we had have turned into reality. I would encourage all entrepreneurs to have a plan in writing and try to stick to it. We read a few books about business plans, how to write them, and what banks are looking for when they read them. We also printed ours on really nice paper with beautiful graphics before we took it to the bank to present to them.

Why You Need a Business Plan— and When

Some experts hold the view that you need a business plan only when you are seeking outside investment or a loan to expand or start your business. While this is certainly one of the main purposes of writing a business plan, it is not the only one. A business plan is much more than a tool for raising capital. First of all, a business plan forces you to evaluate your business idea, to determine whether or not your product or service fulfills a need in the marketplace; in other words, whether the idea is viable as a business at all. Secondly, a business plan gives you a valuable tool for operating your business. Failing to write a business plan at the outset is one of the most frequently cited mistakes entrepreneurs say they have made.

While it is true that some entrepreneurs, even wildly successful ones, do not write business plans, no business can succeed without having a plan, at least in someone's head. There is simply no substitute for thinking your business through on paper. "The experience of writing a business plan clarified my thoughts about my business, made me put them in order and down on paper," says Gail Smith Peterson, the owner of Buckingham Mercantile. "Having it on paper has kept me focused. I keep coming back to it."

> *He who can see three days ahead will be rich for three thousand years.*
> —Japanese proverb

Although there is lots of paperwork involved in owning your own business, the business plan is the single most important document. It's your dream rendered in concrete and offers a chance to think about your business in a deeper way. The process of writing a business plan gives you the opportunity to face the hard and inevitable questions about your business. It is also a chance to anticipate problems down the road and to develop strategies to deal with them before they arise. Finally, a business plan is an essential tool for communicating to others your vision of your company. It is a document you will refer to often, as well as share with potential investors, bankers, potential partners, accountants, employees, and possibly customers.

In general, a good business plan should be twenty-five to thirty pages long, and will take you three to six months to write. It is, of course, possible to write a shorter, less thorough one (a five-page plan is better than none at all), but you will only benefit from a more in-depth analysis of the business opportunity before you. It is also possible to write a much longer one, but conciseness is important as well. If you are writing a plan to raise outside capital, there is no question that you need a comprehensive plan that lays out all of the potential risks and obstacles to success in your chosen business, and the ways in which you think you can surmount them.

It takes work to write a good business plan, but it will save you a lot of unnecessary work later. Those who have gone through the process of writing a business plan wholeheartedly recommend it. There is no downside to this effort. Some parts of the process will be fun, some will be a chore, but all of it will prove immensely useful. Need another reason? Business experts say that there is a higher rate of failure among businesses with no business plan. "What's so good about writing a business plan is that it forces you to make your goals explicit on paper," says Gail Pittman, successful dishware designer. "It makes you realize what goals you have to reach."

Even if you are an inexperienced entrepreneur, a well-thought-out business plan can make the difference between getting start-up funding and not. With no previous retail experience, and not even much of a personal credit history, Pamela Scurry went to the bank with her resume and a business plan and got herself a $10,000 loan to help open her first Wicker Garden store.

What Happens When You Write a Business Plan

When you subject your business idea to the scrutiny of a business plan, two things can happen. The writing of the plan may inspire you even more and convince you that your idea is a winner that you can implement. Or, as sometimes happens, the process of planning and thinking things out may discourage you or make you realize that the business you have dreamed up does not really hold financial water after all. In that case, though it may seem disappointing, it may also be a stroke of luck to avoid what might have been a money-losing proposition.

Some parts of the plan will seem like more work than others. It's a rare person who enjoys crunching all the numbers necessary to make fiscal forecasts, but you might surprise yourself by being one of them. Once you know all the essential elements, there is certainly room for inspiration and even creativity in the writing of a business plan. Like the business itself, the business plan is an expression of you.

Although we certainly recommend that you seek out the advice of experts, associations, and other entrepreneurs on writing a business plan, don't farm out this project. Even if the prospect of writing a business plan makes you break out in a sweat, do it yourself. Once you write your plan, however, it's a good idea to run it by a business consultant or businessperson you respect.

If you don't consider yourself a good writer, don't worry. Good writing is helpful, but not as important as clear reasoning and analysis. If you are using this document to sell your business and appeal to investors or other financiers, they will not be fooled by lyrical turns of phrase. Nor will you. Your business plan is, above all, an extremely useful tool to scrutinize your business idea. It clarifies your destination and offers you a map to guide you there.

It is never too late to write a business plan, which is, after all, a living document to help you manage and grow your business. And every enterprise will benefit from revising its plan periodically to meet the changing reality of doing business. "I suggest updating your business plan every six months," says Christine Dimmick, founder of The Good Home Company. "Ideas and paths change all the time."

You can approach the Small Business Administration for help in writing a business plan, and in doing so increase your chances of getting an SBA-backed loan. But you might want to consider first working with a volunteer business counselor from SCORE, the Service Corps of Retired Executives. SCORE is the voluntary arm of the SBA, and is staffed by men and women who have owned and managed companies and volunteer their time to help fledgling business owners. They know the ropes at the SBA, and can offer invaluable advice on business in general. In addition to the SBA, there are numerous other organizations with web sites featuring downloadable business plan templates as well as other advice. See the Resources section at the end of this book for a listing of some of those web sites.

MY EXPERIENCE WRITING A BUSINESS PLAN

From Debby DuBay, owner of Limoges Antiques in Andover, Massachusetts

Do not let your business plan overwhelm you! Although this document is the backbone of your business idea, it is nothing more than your passion written clearly and concisely on paper.

In my case, I relied on the experts at the Small Business Administration. The SBA has a business plan computer program—you just basically fill in the blanks with your specifics. Their counselors are retirees and volunteers, all of whom have had very successful entrepreneurial experiences, have written several business plans in their lifetime, and are willing to share their expertise with you.

After gathering input and incorporating this data into my ideas for my small business, I put in about a month of intense work on my business plan. At the end of that month I was rewarded with a very well written business plan that is still useful five years later! And, the best part of this story is that my business plan was understood and approved by the same individuals who recommend, financially back, and approve small-business loans.

The Importance of Research

In Chapter One, we talked about the importance of research when you begin to germinate a business idea. Your initial research and more will come into play in the writing of your business plan. Every claim in your business plan will need to be backed up with hard evidence. Pure hype or unsubstantiated claims will not convince anyone of the viability of a business. Enthusiasm alone may win over your family and friends, but facts are needed to persuade people beyond your immediate circle. Investors are looking for a return on their investment. Bankers are looking for loans to be repaid with interest. You owe it to yourself and anyone else who gets involved in your business to know what you are talking about. In the course of your research, you are not likely to find one person or source who has all the information you need. Get used to asking the question, How do I find out about... ?

You will need to read trade journals and everything else you can get your hands on about your chosen field or industry. It is advisable to attend trade shows to observe the trends in your industry and assess the competition. What you learn through this kind of research will help you develop strategies to separate yourself from the pack. These strategies will appear in your plan in a distilled version. There are trade associations for nearly every field, sometimes more than one, and they are generally eager and happy to share data and information about their industries. You can consult the *Encyclopedia of Associations* at your local library to find out about ones relevant to you. Wholesalers and their representatives also can be sources of information. They usually have their fingers on the pulse of their industry. Don't be afraid to ask them questions about trends, what people are buying, and how much they are paying for those items.

For demographic and other information, some useful resources include the U.S. Census Bureau's Division of Population and Housing, the *Rand McNally Commercial and Marketing Guide*, the *Thomas Register of Manufacturers* and *American Demographics* Magazine, from which you can order back issues. The Internet is another valuable tool for research as well.

As always, don't forget to consult other entrepreneurs in your industry, if possible. You may convince an entrepreneur you admire to show you a copy of her business plan. You may also need a more experienced businessperson to guide you through some of the trickier parts of your business plan. As well as consulting SCORE, consult with your local university or college's business school for additional resources and guidance.

You can also pay to have the necessary market research for a business plan done for you. A professional market research firm will charge $2,000 or more, depending on the size of the project. There are also Internet business plan services, but their cookie-cutter templates tend to produce business plans that seem canned.

A Few Words about Format

A business plan should be typed in 12-point type single spaced on 8½ by 11-inch copy paper. Leave white space in the margins and between sections for prospective readers to make notes. Bind it in an inexpensive but clean and professional manner.

The Essentials of a Business Plan

Business plans can vary in complexity, depending on whether you are seeking loans or investors, or just creating a strategy for yourself. But every business plan must convey the basics: What your company is and why it is special; your market; your competition; your marketing strategy; who you are; and financial projections for the next five years.

Here is a more detailed breakdown of a typical business plan:

1. NAME AND ADDRESS OF THE BUSINESS

2. CONTENTS

3. EXECUTIVE SUMMARY

Although it comes first in the business plan, the executive summary should be written last. It is a two- to three-page distillation of the most important points in your business plan, and should be written in such a manner that your reader will want to read more. The lead paragraph is the most important. The first two sentences should be compelling, telling the reader what makes your business special, what important need(s) it fills, and how investors, if you are seeking them, will profit.

The ensuing paragraphs should support that statement with salient points about your management or yourself, market analysis and strategy, financial projections, and information about operating your business. If any of these categories seems mysterious at this point, don't worry. They are explained below.

4. Description of your business

This is actually where you start. And it is a good place to start because it is probably something you've given a good deal of thought to. State and define the overall concept for your business and how it fits into the market. Give the company's mission and reason for being. One way to think about this section is by answering the question, What problem does my product or service solve? Tell about the industry you'll be a part of and whether your business will be manufacturing, wholesale, retail, a service provider, or some combination of these. Give an overview of how your company will be set up.

5. Description of product or service

Another fun section. Detail the product or service you'll be offering and how you will create and deliver them. Use pictures or other visual aids if necessary. If yours is a service company, describe the service in detail. Take the reader through a typical interaction with a client from start to finish.

6. Analysis of the market

This section should address who your customers are, how their needs are currently being met, and how your business will do it better. You will need a thorough analysis of your target customer, including demographic details such as income levels and buying habits. Analyze pertinent demographic trends. You might even consider developing a mythical customer. (For example, she is thirty-five, owns her own home, has 2.4 children and an income of $40,000.) If yours is to be a manufacturing business, you will probably have a variety of customers, from wholesalers to retailers.

Address what niche your business fills. If you can back up any of your claims with actual letters of intent or orders, so much the better. Otherwise, you'll have to rely on market research and market sense.

Explain your pricing structure and how you arrived at it based on standard markup, production costs, and perceived value.

7. Analysis of the competition

You may be tempted to knock your competitors in this section, but you should edit out such comments. Their shortcomings will not necessarily mean your success. An objective analysis of their relative strengths and weaknesses is better. What advantages do you offer? How do your prices compare? Also, project where you can expect competition to arise in the future and how you will handle and keep ahead of it.

8. MARKETING STRATEGY

This section should explain specifically how you are going to reach the market or niche you described in the previous section, and how you will sell your product to them. Some entrepreneurs are tempted to gloss over this section, but it is vitally important. It does not matter how great your product or service is if you have no plan for selling it. For this section, you need to research your options and find out how much each will cost. Will you engage in direct marketing, advertising, promotions, personal networking? Will you send out fliers; attend trade shows; advertise on the radio, in local papers, or in trade magazines? Be prepared to explain why you've selected your particular strategy and how it suits your market. For a new business, an expensive marketing strategy is ill-advised. One that is small and focused, requiring the efforts of only a few people, is more effective.

9. BIOGRAPHIES OF THE PRINCIPALS

Tell about who you are and why you are uniquely qualified to run this venture. If you have a partner or a team in place, tell who they are, what role they will play, how their skills complement one another. Venture capitalists and loan officers tend to pay close attention to this section, so it should inspire confidence.

While this section informs potential investors and funders about your track record, it also provides a chance for you to evaluate your own skills, if you haven't already. It should contain a record of everything you've done that is relevant to your business, written clearly so it can be thoughtfully analyzed. You should include both successes and failures, especially when the failures have increased your capability to run the enterprise. Investors and loan officers are impressed by people who are forthcoming and modest. In other words, don't pad this section. Eventually, the goal is to meet with the people you are directing this plan to, and they are not easily fooled.

10. OPERATIONS

This part is pretty technical. It should describe exactly how your company will operate. Explain in detail your production process from start to finish and where each step will take place. If you are sewing handbags in your bedroom, here is the place to mention it. Then explain how the product will be transported and what backup systems exist. Explain who your suppliers are and whether you have backup suppliers (always a good idea).

11. FINANCIAL FORECASTS

At the most basic level, business is about money coming in, money going out, and the effort to make the first category larger than the second. In this section, you will need to chart and calculate how that is going to happen over the course of the next five, maybe even ten years. This involves some speculation, but it is speculation grounded in reality. You can hire an accountant to help you with these calculations or consult SCORE or your local business school.

First you need to explain where the company currently stands financially and what your overall plan for financing it is.

Step 1 is to establish how much money you have already invested, including personal money, credit-card debt, informal loans; how it has been used and how long it will last.

Step 2 is to figure out how much you need and explain how it will be used. Explain why you need X amount of dollars to start or expand your business.

Step 3 is to lay out a long-term plan for funding. Will growth be funded through profits? Or will there be more than one round of financing?

To describe your current and projected cash requirements, you'll need to calculate your start-up costs as well as your fixed, or monthly, expenses for the next five years.

Start-up costs include the cost of leasing a space; the cost of alterations and renovations; capital expenditures, including everything you need to operate your business, and one-time expenses (opening inventory, fixtures, equipment, signs, furniture, computers(s), fax machine(s), cash register(s), telephone installation).

Fixed, or monthly, operating costs include rent, equipment leases, supplies, utilities, licenses, insurance, salaries, advertising/marketing, distribution, and any others you can think of. After calculating start-up and fixed costs, you may want to add 10 or 20 percent for contingency.

Then there are the projections. For these you need to make educated guesses about your expected sales volume. Be prepared to justify your claims.

As you are charting the amounts of money coming in and going out, you should arrive at certain important conclusions. When do you expect the business to break even? Be profitable? When do you expect a positive cash flow?

This section will make use of two primary kinds of accounting statements that you might as well familiarize yourself with now, since they are vital to the running of a business:

Income statement: Also known as a profit and loss, or P&L, statement, this projects revenues (sales) against expenses. You should project these out for the first five years, monthly until your break-even point, quarterly after that. From these calculations, you will arrive at an annual profit and loss projection, and a cumulative one, when you add them all together. These figures should go into your executive summary.

Balance sheet: This calculates the net worth of your company. To arrive at that, list the company's assets, including investments and equipment. Then list the company's liabilities, including current and long-term debt.

The balance to strike in this section is to be realistic and honest while also showing numbers that would attract investors, who, after all, are in it to make money. Coming close to meeting your projections will be beneficial in the long run and show potential investors or lenders that you mean and can deliver what you say. Raising money is not a one-time thing. You will likely have to do it continually.

Some entrepreneurs create two versions of their financial projections, an aggressive scenario based on robust market demand and a more conservative one based on a weaker performance.

What you highlight in this section may depend on the kind of financing you are seeking. If you are looking for a bank loan, bankers are more interested in the company's fixed assets, like the building and equipment. They want to know that you can offer collateral and guarantee the repayment of the loan at the interest agreed upon. Investors or venture capitalists want to own a piece of your company and its profits. They are generally looking for a big return on their investment, at least 30 percent annually, sometimes more. If you are seeking investors or equity financing, you may need to consult with a lawyer to establish the terms of the investment. Investors will want to know what portion of the company their money will buy, the risks of their investment, an exit strategy, and how many shares you are selling. Being up front about the risks of investing in your business will protect you as well.

It is possible that in calculating your financial projections you'll realize that the company will not be as profitable as you thought or not profitable enough to attract investment. Again this may be disappointing, but it's valuable information to have when there's still time to change strategies. You may opt to start smaller, go slower, and cobble together financing another way, if you still think the basic business idea is sound.

12. APPENDICES

This section will include supporting materials, if you have any: articles about your company, your product, or you; résumés of principals; supporting charts or graphs that do not belong in the main body of the plan.

BUSINESS PLAN DOS AND DON'TS

- Do get yourself started by thinking of your business plan as an extended letter that explains your business idea to an intelligent friend who knows nothing about your particular industry.

- Do write the plan yourself.

- Don't hire someone else to write it. It won't be true to your vision and it won't force you to confront the realities.

- Do show it to a business consultant when you are done.

- Do stay realistic and conservative as possible with your numbers and fiscal forecasts. If you exceed them, it will only reflect well on you.

- Don't change the very nature of your business idea to conform to what you think investors or others might want to hear. If they give you money, you may end up having to start that business instead of the one you really wanted to.

- Don't become so attached to your plan that you fail to recognize and seize unexpected business opportunities that might come along. Don't mistake the plan for the business. Be flexible.

The Mission Statement: Examples

Some business plans include a statement of the company's mission, or aim, in the section where the business and concept are described. This statement, or some version of it, can also serve as a mission statement for the company, and it is an immensely important document for employees, customers, and investors. The mission statement should inspire you and indicate a higher goal than just making money. It suggests that this business can make a positive difference in the world. Christine Dimmick included this paragraph in the beginning of her business plan for The Good Home Company:

OUR AIM

There is a place far in the country that is the home in all of our hearts and dreams. It is surrounded by trees with blue skies and stars as a backdrop. There is a large willow tree that has stood tall for many years, with branches you can swing on. There is a lovely pond to swim in when it is warm and to skate on when it is cold. The grass is the greenest of green and feels like a soft, cool pillow when you walk on it barefoot. Each season brings new pleasures to this special place. The many lilac trees to the side of the home fill the air with sweet perfume every spring. In the summer, the blackberries grow wild by the pond and are plentiful to pick. Juicy red tomatoes on the vine cover the garden along with string beans, basil, and lettuce. A perfect accompaniment to the lemonade and barbecue later that evening. Fall brings the smell of burning leaves and crisp apples, signaling the start of homecoming and family gatherings. The winter air is crisp and the pine trees are covered with the whitest of snow, making the warm fire inside even more pleasurable. Each morning the singing of birds awaken you, and in the summer months crickets sing a sweet song at night. Sunrise brings the smell of fresh-brewed coffee and cinnamon buns and the excitement of daily projects waiting to be accomplished. Fresh-baked treats are always coming out of the oven, and the simple dinners satisfy the hungriest of taste buds. Sounds of children laughing can always be heard and often mingle with the sound of the wind, creating a beautiful and natural chime. Summer thunderstorms are majestic to watch and the hard rain that follows can bring peace to the most cluttered of minds. Wonderful conversation is always in abundance in this home and can often last into the darkness of night. This home knows no difference between family and friends; they are all one and all are welcome. This home is real, and it is our aim to re-create part of it in every product that we make.

Tracy Porter, a designer of beautiful things for the home based in Princeton, Wisconsin, offers the following mission statement which she calls the...

DREAM STATEMENT

Our goal is to be a company that dreams hugely and without limits. A company that turns their dreams into reality by seeking out opportunities that truly tickle our fancy. To inspire ourselves and others. To live a fantasy journey everyday in our business and personal lives. To laugh a lot. To challenge ourselves. To evolve and learn. To prosper so that we can give to others and still eat and drink well, surround ourselves with books, travel, and see the world. To experience an environment that is incredibly playful, stimulating, and encourages growth in all. To share our day to day with people who have wicked good attitudes and an interest in building a brand that stands for fun, integrity, generosity, beauty, fantasy, and approachable deliciousness.

After writing your business plan, you will be so much better equipped—with both a vision and a concrete plan—for the next difficult step: Deciding how to fund your dream and securing the necessary capital.

Financing Your Start-Up Business

Certainly there are lots of things in life that money won't buy, but it's very funny—have you ever tried to buy them without money?

—Ogden Nash

Your business may be a labor of love, but it needs cold, hard cash to enable it to spring to life. In many cases, that money will come from you or from someone very close to you. In fact, more than three-quarters of start-up businesses are financed with the owner's savings, family money, or some other private source. It's not surprising. Banks are conservative, and investors, at least until the recent Internet craze, are often reluctant to back first-time, start-up ventures. There is no denying that in business, just as in life, it is a big advantage to have a financial head start. Even when banks and investors do provide seed money, they usually do so on the condition that the owner has put up a significant portion of her own money first.

But if you don't have the kind of personal resources that will bankroll a fledgling business, there's no need to give up on the idea of starting yours. There is a more favorable entrepreneurial climate and more financial support available for entrepreneurs today than ever before. There are also more options in terms of funding. Banks and investors are looking at businesses owned by women with new eyes. And there are programs in place, particularly within the Small Business Administration, as well as some private groups that try to make up for some of the historical inequities of funding businesses owned by women. In addition, determined and resourceful entrepreneurs have found other, less conventional, ways of funding their business.

Keeping Money in Perspective

No one would sensibly deny that having enough money is vital to the success of any venture, and that undercapitalization is a frequent contributor to business failure. But money is not the only factor that determines the outcome of your company. Creativity, innovation, and resourcefulness are just as vital, if not more so. As Paul Hawken writes in *Growing a Business*, "The major problem affecting businesses, large and small, is lack of imagination, not capital." In Hawken's opinion, too much money is worse than not enough, since it can lead to sloppiness, poor decision-making, and a false sense of well-being. "Just as hunger will make you alert," he writes, "so lack of capital will make you keenly aware of the business environment."

It is better to be comfortable with the money you have, not nervous all the time about making large and onerous payments or having to please investors who do not understand your business. For some entrepreneurs, that means waiting until they can afford to finance their business without putting anyone else's money at risk. Many successful businesses started out small, on a shoestring, grew incrementally, and financed their expansions with profits. This is called bootstrapping, and it's a fine American tradition.

Thirty years ago, Marsha Manchester started Milady's Mercantile, a vintage lace and linens shop in Middleborough, Massachusetts, with a $100 and a box of antique linens a girlfriend gave her. Times have changed since then, but you don't always need a million dollars to start a business. A few years ago, Christine Dimmick, for example, started The Good Home Company with just the $5,000 bonus she received from her job. A few years before that, Rebecca Cole, a garden designer, borrowed $5,000 from a wealthy client in order to open a storefront on a backstreet in New York City selling flowers and garden accessories. She worked out a barter arrangement with the client whereby she was able to pay off the interest on the loan by designing a garden for her patron.

If you have enough savings to pay for your start-up, most experts and entrepreneurs recommend that you start with that, even if it means starting small and growing slowly but steadily. Using your savings does not mean looting the children's college funds, your retirement accounts, or taking out a third mortgage, however. It should be money you've managed to put away for that proverbial rainy day.

Once you can show a track record of profitability, you can approach a bank for a loan from a position of strength. This is exactly what Gail Pittman did when she decided to move her ceramics business out of her home, and got a $10,000 personal loan from the bank to finance the purchase of a new building to serve as headquarters. It was a terrifying but vital move for her, "as scary as if I'd borrowed a million dollars," she says. But it helped her to take herself and her business more seriously and to make the necessary moves to expand it. There is another reason to begin, as early as possible, to take out relatively modest loans. Each small loan you get and pay back improves your credit and makes you a more attractive prospect to lenders.

How Much Do You Need?

It is generally recommended that you start out with enough capital to fund one year of operations. Do a scrupulous job of calculating your start-up costs. Get as accurate a picture as possible of how much your supplies, equipment, labor, insurance, and operating costs will be by calling others in the industry (not competitors, though) to get precise numbers. (A guide to calculating your start-up costs is in the previous chapter, Writing Your Business Plan, in the section on financial forecasts.) It is possible to survive with a bootstrap operation, but being severely undercapitalized puts too much stress on you and will likely put your business in jeopardy.

ADVICE ON FINANCING FROM CLOTHING DESIGNER ISABEL GARRETON

Your resource needs and the scope of your projections—whether you decide to start small, start big, begin with some things in place, or begin with all things in place—will determine your financing. The banking world and institutions such as the Small Business Administration are currently focused on women entrepreneurs. I have found them to be friendly and invaluably helpful. Without hesitation, they will discuss what you want to do, why you want to do it and why you believe you will succeed. Get advice from several people at different banks until you receive the interest and advice you feel comfortable with. They will tell you how to obtain the money you need, what to present in writing, and how to go about it.

Major Financing Options

Whether you invest your own money or someone else's here's a rundown of the major financing options.

PERSONAL MONEY

These are your hard-earned savings, nest eggs, inheritances.

Advantages: You're learning on your own dime, not putting anyone else's money at risk. It makes a certain amount of psychological sense to use your own money to test out your personal dream. If it fails, you won't be in debt to anyone else. And you have an appreciation of the value of your own money that you might not be able to match elsewhere. Using your own money means there are fewer strings attached, no interest to pay back, and no one else owns a chunk of your company. It is an indication that you are willing to put your money where your mouth is, that you have faith in your idea, which is important for you and your future funders to know.

Disadvantages: Starting a business is a risk. You should avoid taking out a third mortgage or raiding the kids' college funds. Also, if you're over thirty-five or forty, it might not be a good idea to liquidate your retirement accounts, as you may not have enough time to build them up again.

MONEY FROM FAMILY AND FRIENDS

A lot of people have used or borrowed family money to start their businesses. The main caveat is to keep these arrangements as businesslike as possible. Make sure your friend/relative/lender knows about the risks of your business. Draw up an agreement in writing that states the amount borrowed, interest rate, and terms of repayment, and make sure everyone understands and is comfortable with those terms. You should absolutely pay back these loans with interest, since the IRS will tax lenders of more than $10,000 to one person at the rate of 6 or 7 percent. Make sure the repayment schedule is one you can meet comfortably without putting your business under undue stress, and in order to avoid resentment on your part. Many relationships have soured as a result of loans that were casually given and even more casually paid back, so don't take any loan that you are not willing to personally repay. As clearly and as politely as possible, make it known that the loan does not entitle your friend or relative to interfere in the operation of your business.

Sisters and partners Margaret and Sallie Jones opened Scriptura, their fine-paper store in New Orleans, with a bank loan and a personal loan from a close friend. "Everyone's situation is different," says Margaret. "We took the only route available to us. However, if you are going to borrow money from a friend, make sure you are very serious in your intent and carefully structure the deal to protect the friendship. Our situation has worked out very well."

Advantages: You don't have to persuade a bank to lend you money.

Disadvantages: Your creditor may feel entitled to have a say in your business. Relationships can become strained.

CREDIT CARDS

This option has tempted many struggling entrepreneurs, but keep in mind that while that $25,000 credit line on your gold card may be convenient, credit cards, with their high interest rates, are an expensive source of cash. You should rely on plastic only if you are confident that the money will soon be rolling in and you can repay quickly. Certainly, it behooves you to shop for a credit card with lower interest rates, but one caveat here: Don't let every lender do a credit check on you. Too many credit checks in a short period of time may look suspicious on your credit record.

Financing a start-up business with a credit card is an option women tend to exploit about three times more than men, according to experts. But there are at least three reasons why a bank business loan is a better choice, if you can get it: The interest rate is a lot lower; bank loan officers are more flexible about late payments than credit card collectors; and credit card debt does not build your business credit track record the way a bank loan does.

Michele Rosier, a floral designer with a flourishing business in Santa Monica, California, says she made things harder on herself by starting her business "by the seat of my pants" and loading up her seven credit cards in the beginning. "It was a bad idea," she says. "Don't do that. It's better to get a bank loan." If she had it to do all over, she says, she'd start with a business plan, a loan, and a budget.

Advantages: Credit cards are convenient and familiar.

Disadvantages: Credit cards are expensive and don't help build a business-credit track record.

OUTSIDE FUNDING

When it comes to outside funding for your business, there are two basic kinds: debt financing and equity financing. Put simply, debt financing is when you get a loan, whether from a bank, friend, or relative, that must be repaid on certain agreed-upon terms, usually in installments over a period of time. Equity financing is when you sell off ownership shares to investors, with whom you then share profits and even some control.

BANK LOANS

There are numerous kinds of bank loans, but they fall into two major categories, business or personal. Most entrepreneurs recommend trying for a business loan first and, if that fails, trying for a personal loan. Even if you get a business, or commercial, loan, you will probably have to personally guarantee it in addition to offering substantial collateral.

Banks are fundamentally conservative and are not in the business of losing money, so be prepared to shop around and expect some rejection. But don't be afraid to ask. Many businesswomen are too intimidated to apply for bank loans. With no previous experience running a business, and a very meager credit history, Pamela Scurry was able to get a loan for $10,000 to help start her Wicker Garden store in New York. She did so on the strength of an impressive résumé (she had been working since she was twelve years old, and, in the years prior to starting her business, had risen fairly high in the corporate world) and a solid business plan.

Even if your business makes all the sense in the world and you already have a strong track record of profitability, you will almost definitely be asked to personally guarantee the loan. This means you'll have to pay it back if your business cannot.

Unless the banker already knows a lot about your business, it is advisable to fill out a thorough loan application and submit it before actually meeting with the loan officer. This will save time and enable him or her to ask more intelligent questions in the interview. Be forthright in the interview. You're not doing yourself any favors if you manage to get a loan under pretenses that don't match the reality of doing business.

Advantages: No one else owns a piece of your company. In the long run, a record of paying back loans will be good for your personal and your business's credit, and will make it easier to get other loans, lines of credit, as well as other banking services for your business, etc.

Disadvantages: You have to keep paying off the debt steadily even when business is slow. Too much debt can hamper the running of your business, make it hard to pay other bills, and, if you fall behind in your payments, impair your credit rating and your ability to raise money in the future. It can be something of a distraction to have to deal with paying loans and loan officers at a time when you should be thinking about building your business.

What Bankers Are Looking For

1. A good credit history: Bankers want to check out your overall attitude toward debt. To check on your credit history beforehand, to make sure there are no unpleasant surprises, or to come up with convincing explanations for lapses, call TransUnion, Equifax or TRW. You may be able to straighten out any errors or misunderstandings before the banker sees them.

2. Collateral: Your company's fixed assets, building, and equipment, or yours.

3. Your personal guarantee on the loan.

4. Evidence that your business can repay the loan: from cash flow statements, projected or actual. It is helpful if you have actual orders and receivables. Lenders are also interested in the quality of your product, the predictable future condition of your industry, and the strength of the overall economy.

5. Equity: The business owner must put in some of her own money, usually 20 to 40 percent of the amount needed. For example, if the business needs $100,000, the owner should put in at least $20,000. Equity is another way of saying the net worth of the business, which is calculated from the balance sheet, a tally of the business's assets and liabilities.

6. Previous experience running a business: It helps, of course, but if you don't have it, you can still try for a loan. Your résumé, if it is impressive, can also help here.

7. A history of profitability: That is, if you have been in business for a while already and are looking for a loan to expand. If you are just starting out, you'll have to show and explain how you expect to make a profit.

8. Up-to-date taxes: Bring your tax returns for the past three years.

TIPS ON DEALING WITH BANKERS

- Shop around for a banker. Invite several to your business or discuss your business with several to see which one has the best feel for it.

- Cultivate a relationship with your banker, even, or especially, when you don't need money.

- Think of your banker as your partner. Once you have been approved for a loan, your banker is as interested in seeing you succeed as you are.

- Be candid with your banker about your goals for your business and the risks. Be open about your cash-flow and performance figures. Share your short- and long-term strategies for growing your business.

SMALL BUSINESS ADMINISTRATION (SBA) GUARANTEED LOANS

Founded to give small entrepreneurs some much-needed support, the SBA is sometimes considered the lender of last resort. An SBA-backed loan is a bank loan with more favorable terms, usually lower interest and a longer repayment schedule. To sweeten the deal for the bank, the government guarantees 75 percent of the loan. An SBA guarantee makes a business that might have seemed risky, perhaps one with few assets, and low cash flow, look a lot more attractive to the average conservative banker. The SBA does not make the actual loan. Local banks and other commercial financial firms that are SBA-approved lending services distribute the loans. You still need to shop around for the appropriate lender.

SBA-backed loans are not for everyone, but they are worth knowing about. Some consider them too bureaucratic, the application process too byzantine, and the approval process too slow. To qualify, businesses must meet certain size restrictions, that vary for different industries and, to some, seem rather arcane. While SBA loan guarantees may not be suitable for every business, there are numerous SBA success stories. Debby DuBay's Limoges Antiques in Andover, Massachusetts, was launched with an SBA-backed loan, and having used the resources of the SBA to plan and fund her business, DuBay has no complaints.

In recent years, the SBA has implemented various programs to speed up the process of applying for a loan and make the process easier to navigate. The SBA directs a substantial amount of its efforts toward minority-owned businesses, with women falling under that umbrella. The Women's Prequalification Loan Program (Pre Qual) was created in 1994 to expedite the application process. With a Pre Qual in hand, you go to the bank with the paperwork done and a loan of up to $250,000 approved. The Low Documentation Program (Low Doc), for loans of under $100,000, is designed to be even more user-friendly. You need only complete a one-page application and your bank completes a one-page analysis of your business, and within 48 hours the SBA will let you know if you are approved.

There are numerous other kinds of SBA loans and programs, including a commercial mortgage, for the purchase, new construction, or refinancing of commercial properties; equipment term loans, for the purchase or refinance of business equipment; permanent capital term loans, which are seven-year repayment loans; and the Greenline Program, a short-term working capital line of credit.

Debby DuBay received an SBA-backed loan to start Limoges Antiques, and recommends the experience to others.

After completion of my business plan, I had no idea how to go about getting financial backing. I didn't even know if I wanted any money and I was shy about seeking outside financing. But, with the encouragement and recommendation from my counselors at the SBA, I decided to take advantage of any and all financing available to me. It was the SBA who sent me to the Reading Cooperative Bank, one of their approved lending institutions, for a low-documentation loans for minorities, which we, as women qualify for. The lending institution does have strict requirements for an entrepreneur seeking funding, but they are based on a sound financial plan and other documents you can easily provide. And for the program I applied for—a low-documentation small-business loan—final approval came from my mentors at the SBA. This entire process was one of the most rewarding and interesting experiences I have had and I highly recommend the use of the counselors, staff, and volunteers at your local SBA. This organization made what could be a very intimidating process simple, fun, and rewarding.

HOW TO MAKE AN SBA LOAN WORK FOR YOU

- Find the right lender.

- Know what your business needs are. Be prepared to explain and justify the figure you are requesting.

- Be ready to provide a complete business plan, or at least background on the principals; history and analysis of the future of the company; owner's financial statements, including tax returns; and monthly cash-flow projections with any assumptions explained.

Advantages: An SBA-guaranteed loan generally offers more favorable terms than a regular bank loan and allows you to keep your ownership interest until your business grows to a point where you want to sell shares.

Disadvantages: Bureaucracy.

EQUITY FINANCING

Some businesspeople do not want to saddle their business with debt, and so they opt for equity financing. In simple terms, equity financing is when you seek investors and sell off agreed-upon portions of the company. This is often a source of financing that a mature company taps, but some start-ups, especially in the high-flying Internet and computer worlds, try to attract so-called venture capital. It is a given that investors, or venture capitalists, are looking for a return on their money. To be attractive to them, most experts agree that a business needs to promise (and be able to justify that promise) a return of at least 30 percent a year. Obviously, not every kind of business can do that, and if you don't want investors breathing down your neck, you might not choose this financing option. It is also possible to seek more patient investors, those who understand that your business may take a little longer to show a return.

If you are going to seek investors and sell off ownership shares in your company, your investors will need to know exactly what percentage of your company their money will buy. Your business plan needs to include all the terms of this arrangement, and you will need a lawyer to help you draw it up.

As in getting a bank loan, seeking investors may involve a lot of rejection. Some experts say you should count on asking one hundred people for every "yes" you receive. Once you do get a few investors, you can use them to open other doors. They have a stake in the success of your company.

Women business owners tend to be more reluctant to seek out venture capital than their male counterparts, according to the National Foundation for Women Business Owners. Given that women entrepreneurs own nearly half the businesses in the United States, it's probably time to start closing that gender gap. To do so, women have to develop more swagger and self-confidence; they have to see themselves as worthy of getting as much money as they can; and they have to cast and comport themselves as leaders. Most venture capitalists are men, so women need to pitch to men in a language that men can understand. Don't frame everything in terms of how women shop; instead you might consider creating a scenario of a man who wants to buy his wife a nice birthday or anniversary present. Do your homework on the venture capital firm you're approaching by studying their web site, and try to network with venture capitalists and people who might know them. As with other areas of professional life, it helps if you can say you have a mutual friend when you make that first phone call. There are also venture capitalist fairs directed at women.

WHAT ATTRACTS SMALL-SCALE INVESTORS TO FUND SMALL BUSINESSES

- A belief in the owner, personally

- A great business opportunity

- The timeliness of a business

- The track record of the owner

- Substantial equity

Advantages: No debt.

Disadvantages: Dilution of ownership. Profits and possibly control may need to be shared. More complicated legal arrangement.

Other Financing Options and Terms

Angels: These are wealthy people who, for their own reasons, enjoy funding and advising businesses, maybe even yours, and offer money on favorable terms.

Irrational investors: A term for people who believe in you and are willing to give you money on extremely favorable terms.

Lines of credit: This provides short-term funds to your business to maintain positive cash flow. Most businesses need a line of credit, which can usually be secured from the bank with which your business has good and ongoing relations.

Letters of credit: A guarantee from the bank that your financial obligations will be honored. Letters of credit are particularly useful when you want to start doing business with a new vendor.

Barter: Barter is another word for trade—either goods for goods, goods for services, or services for services. It is not so much a source of financing as an increasingly useful and widespread tool to consider using while starting up your business, and getting money and other necessities for it under the most favorable terms. It won't work with banks and other institutions, but you may, for instance, negotiate a deal with a private funder, whereby you repay interest on money they've loaned you with bartered services or goods.

Ongoing Financing—Rules of Thumb

Financing your business is not a one-time thing. If your business endures and is successful, you will likely go through several rounds of financing as you expand. Even when you are not actively seeking money for your business, you should be talking to bankers, investors, friends, and anyone else who might provide some capital, about your business and how it is coming

TIPS ON KEEPING START-UP COSTS LOW

- Save money on printed matter, stationery etc. Do you really need to have a business card printed on the most expensive cardstock? Of course, your business card should be distinctive and convey the character of your business, but distinctive does not necessarily mean expensive. Do brochures need to be four-color, or will two colors do? Price out all of your printing needs.

- Save money on equipment. Do you need the most expensive phone system? Is there equipment that you can rent or lease rather than buy? Karen Krasne equipped her Extraordinary Desserts kitchen with items she bought at auction ("Newspapers are always advertising auctions when restaurants go out of business," she says). While her kitchen was inexpensive to set up, she spent her money on the area her customers would see—the tables, chairs, and lighting.

- Save money on services. Are there services your business needs that you can barter for? Cookie Washington, owner of Phenomenal Clothing in Charleston, South Carolina, calls barter the best-kept secret to starting a business. "I have a good friend who is a writer and has done PR. She helped me make a press kit, and I sewed four pillows for her living room. I also barter with my accountant by making her dresses. We are both very happy with this arrangement."

along. From their reactions, you will get a sense whether they might be good sources of capital to tap in the future. As Mary Ella Gabler, the owner of Peacock Alley advises, "Don't hide in your business. You need to be networking all the time with bankers and other people who can help your business. It's hard to remember to take time to do that, but it's so important."

Sylvia Varney, of Fredericksburg Herb Farm, also recommends keeping your money antenna raised. "You need to keep advocating your ideas. And you need to have a nose for money. Then you need the guts to approach people with money."

It is possible, even likely, that if your small business succeeds and slowly grows, bankers and investors will approach you. A rule of thumb in business finance is that money follows money and gravitates toward success. That is what happened to Karen Krasne, who grew her San Diego dessert cafe, Extraordinary Desserts, slowly by cycling her profits back into the business and upgrading gradually. "At first, it was like, thank God somebody bought a cup of coffee," she recounts. But those hand-to-mouth days are long gone. Once the local banks saw how well run her business was, they approached her about financing her expansion with a $25,000 loan.

Another rule of thumb in financing a business is to get money before you actually need it. With time on your side, you can get the best deal and the best terms. Desperation puts you at a disadvantage and will likely be a turnoff to potential lenders and investors.

Finally, once you are up and running, you should think twice about getting a loan to pay for your normal operating costs like salaries or supplies. Something is wrong if the business can't sustain these costs. Rather, consider getting a loan for capital improvements, such as buying a building or investing in a needed piece of equipment. That kind of investment will help your business grow and, in time, pay for itself and then some. In short, the role of financing in business is to help a business blossom and grow, not to subsidize it.

Where and How to Sell Your Product

You have to keep your clients stunned.

—Karen Krasne, Extraordinary Desserts

The moment you decide to start your own business, you have also, like it or not, opted for a career in sales. Sales is an inescapable part of business and an art in and of itself. If you are in the business of making something, whether it's cookies, furniture, baby clothes or pottery, or if you are buying items for resale, like antique jewelry or linens, one of the first decisions you must make is where and how you are going to sell it. The fundamental choice is between direct sales and indirect sales, or retail and wholesale.

In retail, you sell your merchandise directly to consumers. Retail venues include flea markets, catalogues, stores, appointment-only businesses, and web sites. Many businesses these days combine several retail-sales methods. When you sell wholesale, your customers are other merchants and businesses who then sell the goods to consumers. In wholesale, you can generally find the businesses that will buy your goods at industry trade shows or through industry publications. You can also directly approach the buyers for stores and catalogues that you think would be interested in carrying your products.

Where and how you sell your product will depend on what the product is, what kind of a business you want to run, and on your personality, predilections, and style.

All About Retail

Generally, when we think about going into retail, we think about opening a store. But if you are not ready for that big step or don't have the financial resources to rent a space and stock it with inventory, you can start retailing your product(s) on a much smaller, less costly scale. Just about any town has church bazaars, street fairs, crafts fairs, or flea markets. If your product is ideal for a gift, you might investigate renting a table at a fair around the holidays. Another low-cost option is hosting a party, or showing of your wares, at your home, perhaps with other craftspeople. You could also introduce your product at a garage sale. Below are some examples of different approaches *Victoria* entrepreneurs have taken to sell their goods retail:

❖ Paula Gins buys and resells European antique linens by appointment from her home in Littleton, Colorado. She also takes part in several antiques shows a year. She is content to keep her business on this relatively small scale.

❖ Helen Cox, of As You Like It Silver Shop in New Orleans, started out by hosting garage sales out of her home to sell the treasures she collected at thrift stores, flea markets, and other garage sales. Eventually, she realized she needed—and wanted—to open a shop.

❖ Manhattan-based découpage plate designer Mary Nell tested the waters for her wares at crafts fairs, until she finally decided she would target the wholesale market instead. Now she annually exhibits at the New York Gift Show, one of the largest wholesale trade shows.

❖ Gail Pittman, tableware designer, and Leslie Ross, founder of The Thymes Limited, first drummed up interest in their products by hosting shows in rented galleries where people could see, touch, and buy their wares. This solution offered them exposure, feedback, and some cash flow without the commitment of opening a store. Both of these businesses grew into huge enterprises.

Whether you decide to try selling your product at a fair, bazaar, or private showing, the biggest advantage these events offer you is the chance to interact with potential customers to see what they are drawn to and to determine whether there's a market for your wares. "Don't put too much emphasis on how much money you make," advises Mary Nell. "It's more important to gauge people's reactions." Another plus for the entrepreneur who is just starting out and is on a tight budget is that these fairs are a great opportunity for some inexpensive advertising. "If you pass out fifty business cards, and ten percent of those call you to order something, that's pretty good," says Mary Nell.

Not only do you get to learn about your customers at fairs and markets, you also learn about yourself. Do you like this kind of customer contact? Do you like chatting it up with people who happen by? Discovering your own predilections and temperament will help you make an informed decision down the road about whether to open a shop or to sell your product in a less direct way.

You can find a listing of crafts fairs and markets in your area at your local Chamber of Commerce. While you don't need much inventory, and the overhead is low, there are still some costs associated with fairs and markets. You'll need to rent a table or booth from the people running the show. Carting your wares and setting up an appealing selling area also take time, labor, and ingenuity. Make sure to bring colorful signs, flyers, tablecloth/covering; business cards or literature that is specific about what you do, so customers can easily remember and find you; a receipt book and lots of change; and a mailing list sign-up sheet. Eventually, you'll become more selective about the events you attend or decide to move on.

MINDING A STORE

Some people fantasize about owning a shop of their own their whole lives. It's a chance to set up their very own dream space, filled with the things they love looking at and handling, displayed in perfect harmony with their very own taste. Throughout their lives, when they go into the stores owned by other merchants, they take mental notes—unwittingly perhaps—about the little touches they like, the nice package they leave with, how welcome they feel, the window display that first enticed them to go in, how they would do it differently.

While having your own store may be the stuff of dreams, it is also a choice that will anchor your feet firmly on the ground. Shopkeeping is a way of life that deeply grounds you in the community you choose and makes you a visible, even semipublic, figure. The hours are steady and you know where you will be day after day. Quality-of-life issues such as trash collection, road construction, and who your neighbors are will become deeply important to you. Hiring help that shares your sense of mission will be one of your biggest ongoing challenges.

You'll get to know all kinds of people: anyone who happens to drop in, locals, and if you do business in an area favored by tourists, people from all over the world. For this kind of life, liking people and possessing some native savvy and curiosity about them comes in handy. Gail Smith Peterson, whose shop Buckingham Mercantile features her children's clothing designs, has found that the intimacy she has fostered with some of her regular customers is one of the rewards of running her business. She knows their children's birthdays and other life milestones, and they know hers.

June Matheson, former proprietress of the furniture and decorative accessory emporium, Liberty, in Vancouver, says one way she knows she has the right temperament for retail is that she is genuinely interested in her clients' design problems. "I listen to them," she says. "I ask questions."

Some storeowners find that they also spend some of their time educating their customers. Sylvia Varney, of Fredericksburg Herb Farm, says she loves teaching people about the herbs and herbal products sold in the farm's retail outlet. Paulette Knight, owner of The Ribbonerie in San Francisco, is also drawn to the educational aspects of retail. "That's what makes retail fun," she says.

But teaching isn't for everyone. Bookstore partners Cynthia Conigliaro and Joan Gers of Archivia Books in Manhattan teamed up in part because Cynthia has no interest in "baby-sitting" walk-in customers, while Joan has great talent and patience for discovering what customers want. Born shopkeepers love to chat with the browsers and the big spenders alike. So if what you crave above all is solitude, then minding your very own store is probably not for you.

RETAIL LOCATION

In retail, as in real estate, location is critical. When it comes to retail, the volume of traffic is a fundamental consideration. Without traffic—and the right kind of traffic—your chances for success are greatly compromised.

If yours is an upscale product, you need to situate yourself in a neighborhood where well-heeled shoppers go. Some entrepreneurs conduct an in-depth traffic survey and count the number of people who pass a given location, what kind of people, and for what purpose. Season, time of day, and even the side of the street you're on all can affect the traffic volume passing your store, and influence whether those passing by are likely to stop in and buy something from you.

If not in areas of high foot traffic, locations where plenty of cars drive by—but not too fast—can work for many businesses. Ann Fox, of Room Service, says she traded parking for visibility in a location near a well-traveled intersection. Clear signs and good lighting are critical whether you are trying to attract foot or car traffic. Malls and shoppers are an obvious fit, but the cost of space in most successful malls is skyrocketing, and the common area maintenance fees can be prohibitive. It may be that a mall location does not mesh with your aesthetic anyway. With commercial real estate, as with residential, you have to fall in love with the space and see all of its possibilities. "You should walk into the space and immediately want to be there," says Martina Arfwidson, co-owner with her mother, of FACE Stockholm, which has twenty-six store locations worldwide, none of them in shopping malls. "If you want to be there, then customers will want to be there."

Not every store needs a high-traffic location. Specialty stores can generate their own traffic and thrive in more out-of-the-way spots. Paulette Knight's The Ribbonerie in San Francisco is such a store. Knight knew that her customers would seek her out, so she could locate her shop in the much less expensive wholesale district of that city. "People come," she says, "because they specifically want what we have."

While traffic and visibility are important, they need to be balanced with an affordable rent, otherwise you'll be working for the landlord rather than for yourself. One rule of thumb is that your rent should be about 10 percent of your sales. Another way to calculate what you should spend is that your rent should be about 4 to 5 percent of your total operating costs.

For those who cannot afford to pay the steep rents of the more fashionable addresses, it may be worth exploring areas where economic development incentives are offered. Perhaps your city or town has a federal Main Street Revitalization Zone, a program designed to promote retail on many of the nation's main streets. To find out if there are any such programs in your area, contact your local Chamber of Commerce.

Being willing to go a little off the beaten path sometimes pays off handsomely for merchants. Pamela Scurry rented the only Madison Avenue address she could afford for her first Wicker Garden store, many blocks north of the area most shoppers ventured. "I figured, as long as I had a Madison Avenue address, my customers would hop in a taxi, and keep going until they found me," she says. These days, Madison Avenue in the 90s has blossomed into a hot and desirable shopping district, and Scurry was once named "retailer of the year" for her part in that flowering.

Monica Schaeffer also started on a limited budget in an out-of-the-way location. She bought a building in Wakefield, Rhode Island, a town that had seen better days, to house her store, Wild Child. When the economy improved and the town's fortunes lifted, she was sitting on a tidy little real estate investment. Her store and that investment not only financed her children's college educations, they financed her next exciting business move into clothing design.

LOCATION ADVICE FROM ENTREPRENEURS

> Locating your business in the right spot is very important. We chose to put our store in a well-traveled area of town, situated on a block surrounded by coffee shops and other intimate boutiques where there was great pedestrian traffic of both locals and tourists. When you first open and don't have an established clientele, it is helpful to rely on the success of those around you.
>
> —Margaret Jones, Scriptura,
> fine-paper and stationery, New Orleans

I had the cutest storefront in my downtown on a very busy three-intersection road with 5,000 cars going by daily. I left window spotlights on at night to find notes slipped under the door from the previous night from anxious buyers. I didn't have to advertise; word of mouth spread like wildfire.

—Marsha Manchester, Milady's Mercantile,
antique linens, Middleborough, Massachusetts

I highly recommend opening your store in a freestanding location rather than in some high-priced center. The fees in these centers (called common area maintenance or CAM fees) can add as much as $10 a foot to your rent. You have to ask yourself if being located in one of these centers will provide enough additional traffic to make it worth all the extra money. If you open a store in a freestanding location, you can control your own destiny.

—Ann Fox, Room Service,
floral-themed home furnishings, Dallas

Choosing a Spot—Step by Step

1. Have a general idea of what you are looking for, how much space you need, how much you can afford to spend.

2. Find a knowledgeable realtor and get to know the market thoroughly. Be sure your expectations are realistic.

3. Take the following into consideration when evaluating locations:
   - visibility
   - square footage
   - size of display window(s)
   - parking
   - affordability
   - room to expand
   - insurability
   - local building and health codes
   - storage space
   - signage
   - amenities
   - adequate wiring and plumbing

4. Before beginning any sort of lease negotiations, try to choose several possible locations, ranking them in order of preference. Having a backup gives you a stronger negotiating position.

5. Since lease negotiation usually involves compromise, decide in advance what you can and cannot live with. What is your minimum square footage? What is your maximum? Make a list of what you'd like to see on the final lease. Be ready to walk away if the terms of any lease are unacceptable.

NEGOTIATING A LEASE

Negotiating a store lease can take a long time. To smooth the way, it is a good idea to hire a real estate attorney, but not one who is so overqualified that he won't give your lease negotiation the attention it needs. You don't need the best attorney in the country, just a competent one. Make sure you know in advance what your attorney will be charging you, and bear in mind that virtually everything on a lease may be negotiable. Here are some items to scrutinize on your lease agreement or retail store agreement:

- Length of lease: Remember to take your growth expectations into account.

- Escalation clause: How much rent will go up with inflation.

- Use clause: Try to get as broad a use clause as possible. This will give you flexibility in terms of what you sell and in subleasing the space.

- Renewal option: The option to renew at the original rent. Try to get an option to renew for the longest span possible.

- Maintenance: All responsibilities should be spelled out down to minor items like who will provide copies of keys.

- Heating and air conditioning: How will you be charged for these utilities? Do your research and find out from at least two sources what kinds of expenses you can expect.

- Additional charges: Make sure that real estate taxes, common area charges, and other additional fees are proportional with your square footage and that you are not paying more than your share.

- Free rent: Make sure you negotiate for adequate rent-free time while you are building your store. Be sure you know how long it will take to build it and that you can start building right away. Try to get as many months free as possible. Some lease agreements will state that rent must be paid as soon as construction is done.

- Signing bonus: Simply, a break in the rent. Another incentive. See if you can get one.

FINDING THE RIGHT MERCHANDISE: DEALING WITH SUPPLIERS

In addition to dealing with customers, a large part of a shopkeeper's time is spent finding and buying inventory for her store. This means cultivating relationships with manufacturers, wholesalers, and other vendors, attending trade shows, going on buying trips and ferreting out interesting but little-known suppliers, learning about pricing, and making sure that a store down the street is not selling the same items you are and for a few dollars less.

Manhattan jewelry dealer Camilla Bergeron says that finding the right antique jewelry to sell in her store is the hardest part of running her business. "If you find a good supplier," she says, "lock onto him. When suppliers show you stuff you don't like, be diplomatic. Tell them it's not your look, so nobody will waste their time or yours."

As in many aspects of business, finding and dealing with suppliers and vendors is all about relationships. The best way to maintain good relations with vendors is to pay them promptly. When you are first starting out, vendors who do not know you will require payment in advance or on delivery. As they get to know you as a reliable payer, you may establish terms with them and pay within thirty days. If you become known as a person who pays her bills promptly, suppliers will more likely contact you when they have an exciting new item for sale and give you the kind of fast service that may make or break your business. Shopkeepers need to be aggressive in finding suppliers. The best way is to attend trade shows and meet them face to face.

Contracts between suppliers and their outlets are practically nonexistent in the home furnishings and decorative industries. You should certainly try to secure verbal assurances of exclusivity or a guarantee that a supplier won't sell the same item to your competitor down the street. "I've found that if they aren't going to be loyal to you, you're better without them," says Ann

Fox of Room Service. You also need to establish terms with them. At first, they will require you to pay on delivery, which leaves you little recourse if an item arrives broken or damaged. Eventually, you can negotiate better terms.

If lean times come and you have trouble paying the bills, don't hide from your creditors, advises Wicker Garden's Pam Scurry. "If you're in the soup," she says, "be honest about it. There were times when I'd pay $50 toward an invoice, and write on the check, 'More to come! Thanks for your patience!'"

Even when you have all the vendors and suppliers you think you need, keep a file of possible alternatives. Solicit price lists and catalogues from possible vendors to have on hand if one supply source dries up.

BALANCING CHANGE AND STASIS

Shopkeepers must learn to maintain the balance between continuing to carry the same reliable items and giving repeat customers new things to look at and buy. "People come back and want to know what's new," says Sylvia Varney of Fredericksburg Herb Farm. "You can't just keep still. People will demand that you grow."

When you are selling items that are rare, like antiques, your inventory is likely to shift all the time. "My customers often ask for an item they saw in the store before," says June Matheson, of the antiques emporium Liberty in Vancouver. "I tell them to always pick up the pieces they like when they see them because we don't reorder anything. It's always new merchandise." Another reason to keep moving is to stay one step ahead of copycats, an annoyance that just about every successful business contends with at some time or another.

DISPLAY WITH FLAIR

How you display what you sell can be as important as what you are actually selling. More than ever, shopping has become a form of entertainment, and the ability to create eye-catching window displays that entice shoppers to buy is a highly prized skill. Successful shopowners recommend that you change your in-store and window displays frequently, every two weeks is best, but don't let more than a month go by. Karen Krasne, whose Extraordinary Desserts sells objects she finds all over the world on shopping trips as well as great desserts, offers this seemingly simple piece of advice: "You have to keep your clients stunned."

Some women are drawn to retail because they know they have a knack for arranging and rearranging things in an appealing way. Carol Bolton capitalized on her talent for putting flea-market finds together in her six-shop empire in Fredericksburg, Texas. She knew how to arrange objects so that they resonate and tell a story, becoming something altogether new. With each display, she shed fresh light on the decorative possibilities of any given object. The way a blanket is thrown over a chair, tea cups are stacked, postcards are arranged, or blouses are paired with skirts may provide a visual clue to potential buyers of how that particular item would look on her or in her home.

It may be that an item is not moving because of how it is displayed, in which case you will have to experiment with rearranging, learning as you go

TIPS ON DISPLAY

- Your window display is a kind of advertising. Consider spending more on it in lieu of paying for ads. Make it memorable and attention getting.

- Inside your store, use all the available space, but avoid clutter, so that customers can easily get to items that interest them and you can keep the store clean.

- Clothing racks should be user-friendly, at the right height, and not too crowded. Sometimes less is more.

- Furniture and decorative accessories are best displayed in a way that lets people know how they would look in a real home. Set up a room, a vignette. Imagine the person who lives in that room down to every last detail. What book would she or he be reading? Make it consistent.

- Place pretty, small impulse items near the cash register. Some shoppers may not want to buy much, but don't want to leave empty-handed.

- Rotate the displays when things get slow and seem a little stale.

- Remember, everything in your shop contributes to the overall feel. Flowers, chimes on the door, etc. Obsess on the details.

along. "You have to be constantly merchandising your store," says Kate Flax, of Kate's Paperie. "We are constantly moving things around, rearranging, showcasing different items. The public finds it exciting. I've heard that people, when they are depressed, like to walk past our store at Seventy-third Street and Third Avenue. It cheers them up."

Martina Arfwidson of FACE Stockholm prizes a crisp, clean look that makes shopping easy for the customer. "Everything has to be delicious," she says. The smells, the fresh flowers, the uniformly black pens in a spotlessly clean glass jar on the register. "My mother runs her finger along every surface when she comes into a store. The stores have to be perfect. Good is not good enough."

THE LITTLE TOUCHES

One piece of wisdom about owning your own business that bears constant repeating is to imagine yourself as the customer. Nowhere does this apply more than in the case of running a store. Think: How do you like to be treated in a store? What have been some of your more memorable shopping experiences? What are the little touches that make one store a place you want to return to again and again? Attractive gift wrapping, intriguing music wafting through the store, an atmosphere that is warm and welcoming, helpful but not pushy sales people, unique shopping bags all contribute to a customer's desire to linger, return, and send her friends.

> We want people to enjoy coming to the shop. We offer soft drinks, chairs and magazines for husbands to read while their wives shop. We do not charge for gift wrapping and we have nice silver bags with rope handles to give to customers who buy silver and take it with them. We even give our customers a sample bottle of silver polish, which does not cost a lot, but people are ecstatic when we hand it to them. On occasion, we have taken people to their hotels if a taxi does not show up. At the end of each year we send our best customers a special gift. We answer the phone after hours (a real person to talk to). On top of all these extras, we also manage to keep the prices within reason.
>
> —Helen Cox, As You Like It Silver Shop, New Orleans

Every little detail affects your customers' experience, from the design of the tags on the clothing, to the satin ribbon on the gift box, to the pitcher of ice water with sliced lemons there for the taking. Some of the details are as intangible as they are important. Your customers will be influenced by the quality of light in the store, and the lack of dust in the corners, the fresh clean smell of the air without, perhaps, even knowing what is hitting them.

OTHERS WHO MIND THE STORE

Most retailers agree that finding good staff is one of the most difficult parts of their business. In retail, salaries are generally low, and finding people who share your sense of dedication and mission but who do not have the same stake in the success of the business you do is practically impossible. High turnover is all too common, and theft is a chronic and painful problem that needs to be factored in. "We've tried everything from bored housewives to high-priced stylists," says Linda Wade, owner of Putti, a furniture store in Toronto. "Both are problematic. Our best success has been with enthusiastic young people."

We will delve more deeply into staffing issues in Chapter Ten, but any would-be storeowner should know that finding and keeping help will be one of her greatest challenges.

RETAIL AS PART OF THE BUSINESS

Even if your ultimate desire in life is not to own and run a store, a retail location can figure into your overall business plan. For designers of all kinds of goods, a store is a showcase, a public stage where they can exhibit their personal sense of style. Manhattan-based garden and floral designer Rebecca Cole realized early on that she needed a way to show her designs, and her shop, Potted Gardens, became one part of her multifaceted business, selling antique garden accessories, containers, and flowers, and also serving as headquarters for her design service. Six years later she phased out the store in order to focus her energies on designing and on becoming a media personality, offering tips on lifestyle and gardening.

Many furniture designers will open a "prototype store," which shows other retailers how they envision their furniture being displayed. For designers in general, opening a store can be part of an overall strategy to gain exposure and a following, so that when you take your business in another direction, like wholesale or direct mail, customers will follow. Or, like the rug designer Claire Murray, you may opt to maintain your retail operation while wholesaling your products and licensing your designs as you expand your empire.

RETAIL BURNOUT

While some entrepreneurs find that keeping shop is a way of life they enjoy over the long haul, others reach their saturation point far more quickly.

Vanessa Noel, the Manhattan-based shoe designer, began her business with a highly visible Madison Avenue location. When she finally closed the store and opened a showroom instead, she felt liberated. She compared having a retail location to "having a baby cemented to the sidewalk." For a young woman still in her twenties and eager to have some semblance of a social life, retail was not the life for her.

Floral and clothing designer Monica Schaeffer also found that she was ready to move away from retail after seven years. Her store, Wild Child, an offbeat floral design store in Rhode Island, had taken her further than she had ever dared to hope.

Mickey Kelly and Susan Kelly Panian, sisters who started the successful mail-order company Whispering Pines, featuring "things for the cabin," began their business with two stores, one in Piermont, New York, and another in Delray Beach, Florida. When the two women came down with a simultaneous case of retail burnout, they took the company in a new direction that proved even more successful—a mail-order company based in Fairfield, Connecticut. The stores had launched them, building a huge base of customers eager to be on their mailing list for a catalogue. Without the stores, the business might never have taken off.

A store can also anchor a business that does a lot of its selling by mail order or over the web. A flagship store in the historic district of Charleston Gardens, in Charleston, South Carolina, is part of the overall strategy of Charleston Gardens, which sells garden accessories and furniture. "When people experience the store, there's an understanding of the quality and service of our business," says Leeda Marting, the founder and owner. "It makes us more trustworthy."

FROM WHOLESALE TO RETAIL

For some entrepreneurs, like Paulette Knight, who was born into a family of sewers and has a special passion for ribbons, selling retail is the logical next step on their business journey. For thirteen years, Knight imported special items like French wired ribbon, selling it wholesale and making a nice living at it. Four years ago, she thought she spotted an opportunity in retail. For one thing, the disappearance of notions departments at department stores had left a gap in the retail landscape that she knew she could fill. "Starting to retail was a given," she says. "It wasn't like starting from scratch. I already had the inventory and the wonderful museum-quality antique ribbon cabinets to display it." Now that she has started her store, she loves it. Retail is a lot more fun than wholesale, she says. "It's more hands on, more show-and-tell."

But not every product flows naturally from wholesale to retail. "It should be something unique," says Knight, "and it should be something that manufacturers sell in bulk, but consumers want in smaller quantities."

Selling Wholesale

If you design and make one or more products on a large enough scale and are interested in broader, less personal marketing, you may decide to sell your wares wholesale. This means you will sell to other merchants, who, in turn, will sell your product at a somewhat higher price to the public. While there is more freedom and flexibility in wholesale, you also have less control over how your product is displayed and sold. Although it might seem that the more distribution points for your product, the better, it is wise to be selective about who carries your product.

The two fundamental ways of finding buyers to carry your product are to participate in industry trade shows or to make appointments with the people who make buying decisions at the stores or catalogues in which you envision your product being sold. Eventually, you may even contract with a sales rep, who will sell your product, along with those of other manufacturers, to stores in a particular region, usually on a straight commission basis.

Initially, and until you are well established, you may even have to get out on the road and show your product to buyers you think might be interested. Jane Goodrich, who started Saturn Press, a greeting-card company in Maine, initially traveled around with a guest book she had made, showing it to regional stores and small inns. "It wasn't fun," she says, "but you have to do it. It helped get the product out there."

If there is a store in which you think your product should be sold, consider calling the merchandising manager or buyer, and make an appointment to show your wares. If you can't get an appointment, ask the buyer where he or she does the buying for the store. Buyers in the industry you are trying to enter are invaluable sources of information.

TRADE SHOWS

There is at least one trade show in just about any industry, so first you need to find the one that is appropriate to yours. Some of the big ones are the annual home furnishings show in Highpoint, North Carolina, and the annual New York Gift Show. To find out about the trade show for you, contact your industry's trade association. You can also contact your local convention center to find out which trade shows it hosts. Trade shows are not merely chances to sell product and line up orders, they are incredible networking opportunities where you will meet everyone from sales reps, to web-site designers, to suppliers of business essentials like boxes and bags. The downside is that it can be difficult for a new business to participate in trade shows. Many have waiting lists. The New York Gift Show, for example, has a waiting list of several years.

Before you rent a booth or a showroom (usually at a cost of $3,000 to $5,000), you should attend the relevant trade show to get a sense of what goes on, how people display their wares, and what kind of competition you'll be up against. Participating in a trade show can be an expensive proposition, so you'll want to make the most of the ones you attend. When you do attend one, you may discover ways to cut down on costs. To save money at her first trade show, Cookie Washington, the Charleston, South Carolina, wedding dress designer and maker of the "Kiss Bag," first chose one within driving distance. The Atlanta Apparel Mart had the added bonus of taking place in a town where she had friends who put her up. She also cut costs by sharing a showroom with a jewelry designer.

There are always stories of people who hit it big at their very first trade show, taking orders beyond their wildest dreams or expectations. Potter Karen Skelton attended her first New York Gift Show almost as a lark, at the urging of a friend from a pottery class. At the show, she took in orders for 7,000 pots, which sealed the deal. She left her corporate graphic arts job, and opened a ceramics studio upstate in Accord, New York, and frantically worked to fill the orders. In the early days, she often had to rely on the patience of the merchants who had ordered pieces from her. Designer Tracy Porter drew a similarly overwhelming response at her first sojourn to the New York Gift Show, returning home to Princeton, Wisconsin, with $74,000 worth of orders, after she and her husband and business partner, John, had barely scraped up the $5,000 they needed to attend. The Porters worked round the clock to fill the orders, and their business, Stonehouse Farm Goods, was launched as a result.

The more likely scenario, however, is that at your first wholesale trade show, business will be pretty slow. Good Home Company founder Christine Dimmick says she took about $78 worth of orders at her first show. Newcomers often do not get the most desirable booth locations. And often, buyers prefer to do business with someone who has been around for a few

TIPS ON TRADE SHOWS

- Have a clear goal when you attend a trade show, whether it's a particular sales figure you want to hit, finding a sales rep, or networking. At the same time, be flexible so that you can seize opportunities that arise that may not have been part of your plan.

- Make your booth visually appealing, like a store window. If your product is not beautiful on its own, consider having props (but make sure they don't overshadow your product). Bring fabric or other table dressing and one clear sign. Your booth should impart the flavor of your business and, after a number of years, should be recognizable to those who follow you. Don't make your booth too cluttered. Buyers want to move quickly at trade shows—there's a lot to see—and if your booth looks like it will be too time-consuming, they may pass it by.

- Don't pretend to know what you don't know. Ask questions. If you are not familiar with the shop the buyer represents, ask him or her about it. What kinds of things do they carry? Who are their customers?

- Require a deposit on orders to pay your expenses, whether you are importing the merchandise or making it.

- Be realistic and honest about how long it will take you to fulfill orders. If you run into a problem, communicate with the buyer about any delay. People really appreciate honesty and chances are they'll understand.

- Remember, even if you don't sell much at your first few trade shows, the feedback on your product from people in your industry is still valuable.

years, someone they know has a solid operation. You may get a lot of inquiries and interest, but not very many orders, until buyers see you a few years running.

FINDING GOOD SALES REPS

Among the people you'll meet at trade shows are wholesale sales reps. These are professional sales people who usually represent a group of similar or complimentary products, which they try to place into stores in a given region. This can be a tremendous relief to a creative person who wants to focus on design and manufacturing rather than selling. Sales reps also work on a straight commission basis, usually 10 to 20 percent, so having a sales rep does not mean paying an additional salary.

You can also seek out sales reps on your own, but some say it's better if the sales rep comes to you. "Then you know they're really excited about your product, and chances are they'll do a better job for you," says Jane Goodrich of Saturn Press greeting cards.

Although it can be very flattering to be approached by a sales rep, Goodrich also recommends being selective. "Sales reps come and go," she says. "I'd rather have ten of them doing a really good job, than fifty whom I don't really know that well. When a sales rep approaches me, I ask to see her other lines. I want to see that she is repping things of similar quality, that our cards are a good fit."

Mail Order

Before the World Wide Web exploded on the scene, mail-order catalogue businesses were widely considered the wave of the shopping future. They remain popular. Even many e-businesses have decided to bolster their marketing with catalogues. The staggering success of companies like L. L. Bean, Smith and Hawken, and White Flower Farm inspired many to jump on the catalogue bandwagon, but most quickly went out of business. Too many would-be merchants saw mail order as a way to quick riches, but, like any other business, those that sell by mail require care, passion, commitment, a niche, and talent.

Mail order, like e-business, offers convenience to the shopper, who can view pictures of products in her home and make buying decisions without ever stepping outside. With catalogues and web sites, as opposed to bricks-

and-mortar businesses, long-distance shopping becomes possible. Your customers are not limited to the people who physically come to your store, whether by happenstance or intention.

From the point of view of the merchant, there are some similarities in the way catalogues and web-site businesses operate. Both are retail operations without the need for a well-located store. You must produce either an eye-catching piece of print literature (in the case of mail order) or an attractive web page (in the case of web sites) that presents your products in a positive and accurate light, conveys the overall feel and quality of your business, and also gives customers a convenient way of ordering. If you or others involved in your business have talents in writing, photography, or graphic design, you should certainly use them. If not, you will need to hire outside experts to produce your catalogue or web site. Then there is the fulfillment side of the business. You need a warehouse or an ironclad agreement with your suppliers, a system for taking orders, and a method of quick and reliable delivery.

There are also some important differences between mail order and web-based businesses. Mail-order catalogues are direct marketing to carefully chosen prospects, whereas a customer must actively seek out a web site. Web sites are in some ways more akin to traditional retail, albeit in cyberspace. People tend to use the web to search for a specific item that they already have in mind, whereas, catalogues present existing items in hopes of sparking someone's interest in buying them.

It can be difficult to launch a mail-order business from scratch, so many businesses first build up a following with retail stores to springboard their way into mail order. Mickey Kelly and Susan Kelly Panian, the sisters who started Whispering Pines, a catalogue of country items, first built a customer base with a couple of stores. Because their customers frequently expressed the desire to keep buying things from them long distance, through the years the sisters compiled a mailing list that became the core of their target mail-order market. Many businesses also combine traditional retail with catalogue and web shopping (think Pottery Barn). Charleston Gardens also uses its flagship store as a way to collect names for its mailing list, as well as to give customers a way to assess the quality of the store. Their web site also generates names for the list.

Although you won't have to pay the rent for a store in an all-mail-order business, there are plenty of other start-up costs, including production costs, design costs, the cost of buying the right mailing list from a list-broker, postage, storage space, toll-free numbers, and people to answer the phones, wrap, and ship things. Many businesses with catalogues charge a fee for sending it, which is then discounted from a purchase. Predicting volume is perhaps one of the trickiest parts of both mail-order and web-based businesses. Too little volume is obviously a problem, while too much volume can leave you bleary-eyed and overwhelmed. The Kelly sisters still remember the enormous response they received to their launch, which required that they recruit every family member and friend they could to take orders and pack merchandise.

Many merchants start small, with inexpensively produced brochures containing just a few items that they send to customers who have expressed a strong interest in buying their wares. Printed material and some direct-mail marketing should be a part of any business's marketing plan. Producing and printing a catalogue can be expensive. You need one that stands out from the pack, since consumers are inundated with such literature. Every design decision—the quality of the photos or drawings, the paper stock, the wording of the copy, the size of the package— requires careful thought. Your catalogue is your ad, your store, and your sales force all in one.

WHAT MAKES A GOOD CATALOGUE

- Design that separates it from most of the mail consumers get. The catalogue for Whispering Pines is printed on creamy white, linen-textured paper and has won awards for its graphic design. Archivia Books prints its catalogue with black-and-white photos, and the booklet is an unusual square size and shape.

- Interesting copy that makes the benefits to consumers clear. A personal and friendly writing style is recommended since direct mail is, to some extent, reminiscent of a personal letter you are writing to your customer.

- Photos or illustrations that convey the real quality of the product. Customers don't like to be misled. And if the real item looks nothing like the picture, they may insist on returning it.

- Easy ordering procedure. A 24-hour toll-free number, fax number, and e-mail address are all recommended. Offer a variety of convenient payment options.

CREATING AND MAINTAINING A GOOD MAILING LIST

A mail-order business will stand or fall on the quality of its mailing list. It does not matter how great your product is or how brilliant your catalogue, if it is not going to the right people, those efforts are wasted and your cost of sales will be untenably high. Print is an expensive medium, and you don't want to waste your efforts on low-probability buyers. Start cultivating a mailing list the moment you begin getting your product out there. If you attend craft or trade shows or have a store, keep a register for people to sign their names and addresses (and e-mail addresses.)

If you buy a list from a listbroker, be sure to question the broker closely and invest in one that is targeted to your market, whether it is newlyweds or women over forty earning at least $60,000 annually. If you buy a list from another catalogue company, be sure that its market is similar to yours.

Maintenance is important. Periodically, clean out your mailing list. Customers move and sometimes die. (To your customer, it can be annoying, if not downright painful, to continue getting mail for a loved one who is deceased.) If appropriate, you might want to keep additional information on your customers, like their children's birthdays, their wedding anniversary, etc. If people call and ask to be on your mailing list, ask them where they heard about you. It will give you a good idea of what are your most effective ways for reaching customers.

To weed out the browsers from the serious customers, some mail-order companies charge for their catalogue, especially when the literature is expensive to produce. Then when someone orders an item, you can deduct the payment for the catalogue.

Web Sites and E-Business

The Internet is such a fascinating landscape and one that we are committed to learning about. We use our web site as a convenience for our customers to learn, be inspired, shop, and experience what our company is all about. It is a tool that has unlimited possibilities, like leading our customers to stores near them and helping expose our designs to manufacturers who have an interest in creating partnerships with our company.

—Tracy Porter, housewares designer, Princeton, Wisconsin

It is impossible to escape the fact that personal computers, the Internet, and the World Wide Web are transforming the way people shop, live, and do business. Clearly, this technology is here to stay. American consumers have tasted the convenience that online shopping affords them, and found it very much to their liking. That doesn't mean that they never again want to set foot in a real shop, touch and smell things, and talk to shopowners; it just means that they are likely to do some of their shopping in the virtual world as well. For merchants, the web also offers numerous advantages. Not the least of these is that space on the World Wide Web, unlike in the world of concrete, steel, and flesh, is virtually free. No rents, no landlords.

Web sites have the additional advantage over catalogues and printed material of being easier and quicker to maintain and update, and are instantly available to anyone who is interested in learning more about your business. When someone calls (or e-mails) and says, "I'm interested in learning more about your business. What do you sell?" nothing beats the immediacy and the ease of simply referring them to your web site. As clothing designer Isabel Garreton says, "I believe that any business should consider a web site today." Hers is an opinion that is widely shared. Just about any business will benefit from some sort of web presence and strategy. The question is what kind? There are several options:

1. *Simple e-mail:* Set up an e-mail account under your business's names; for example, jane@janesdesigns.com. You can set up an e-mail account like this with any of the hundreds of larger Internet service providers (ISPs).

   Even if you are not ready to mount a web site, you should consider registering for a domain name (e.g., www.yourbusinessname.com). This will ensure that no one else can mount a site by that name for a certain amount of time. If the domain name you want is not available, choose one that gives a clear idea of what you are selling and what your business is about, perhaps your company's slogan. Domain name searches are free and the cost of registering a domain name (through Network Solutions, the largest web domain name registry) is minimal: $70 for the first two years, $35 for each additional year.

2. *A web site that publicizes and advertises your products:* A relatively simple site, this would probably include pictures of products and prices, as well as some background information on your company.

3. *A transactional web site:* This is the most complicated option. You will need to set up an online merchant account with your bank, credit card processing, and include shopping cart software so that clients can shop. You will need to hire a web designer to build and design your site at

$50 to $100 per hour and a web maintenance person for $80 to $150 per hour. Plan on updating your site at least once a week.

DEVELOPING YOUR WEB STRATEGY

How do you decide what kind of web strategy is right for your business? "Ask your customers and clients what kind of web site would help them do business with you," says Jane Applegate, CEO of SBTV.com and a small-business guru. "It's amazing how many people don't do their homework to find out what their customers want." Needless to say, if your customers are not online users or web shoppers, an elaborate web site for your business may be a waste of money, time, and effort.

Once you have an idea of what your customers want, visit as many web sites as you can of similar businesses and competitors as well as other businesses, and get a sense of the depth and range of options. You may also want to read about the subject of web design.

The cost of setting up a web site can vary widely. For do-it-yourselfers, there is software that enables you to do it for a pittance. Most business experts recommend that you hire a professional web site developer or producer to execute yours rather than asking your best friend's baby-sitter's cousin, who just happens to be good with computers. Research the producers and developers of web sites you like and admire. You may also be approached by web site designers at trade shows or in the course of

WHAT TO LOOK FOR IN A WEB PRODUCER

- Choose a company that is more than a one-man shop (it is hard for one person to stay up with all the latest trends) but not too big. You will need to have an ongoing and direct relationship with your web producer.

- Look at the producer's web site and ask to see its web portfolio. You are looking for visual appeal and ease of navigating around the web sites to look at products, to order, and to make transactions.

- Find out if the company has won any awards for its web designs or if it has any testimonials from clients or business associations.

- Find out what other services the company offers in addition to web design. Are services such as copywriting, marketing, or advertising, and web site maintenance available?

TIPS ON WEB SITES

Source: www.onlinewbc.org, the Small Business Administration's web site for women-owned businesses.

- Before you meet with the web producer you choose, do some planning. Create a diagram of the web site you want. Include how the pages of your web site will be linked.

- Your home page should feature your logo, a simple graphic, and perhaps a caption. The home page is the first thing your customers will see, so it should be inviting, not take too long to load, and convey your company's mission.

- Include a street map to your web site for ease of navigation.

- Use links judiciously. Don't make it too easy for customers to leave your web site.

- Invite feedback from customers. Put a link to your e-mail on every page. Consider putting a message board on your site. Make it easy for customers to communicate with you. Try to respond promptly to e-mail sent by customers. The web offers a chance to create surprisingly intimate little communities by virtue of its interactivity.

- To reduce loading time (the amount of time it takes for your site to appear on a viewer's computer screen), use postage-stamp-sized graphics that people can click on to enlarge.

- Make sure it is easy for search engines to find your site. (Your web site designer should know how to embed codes that search engines will use.) Make sure to submit your site to Yahoo, the largest Internet portal. Other portals include AltaVista and HotBot.

- If yours is a site for transactions, include shopping cart software, make sure you get a secure site for Internet sales. You need to be able to allay customers' fears about credit-card transactions over the Internet and make it as easy as possible to purchase from your web site.

- Put your web address and e-mail address on all of your literature and advertising. It also should appear on your business card, shopping bag, and stationery.

doing business. Be choosy. The right web producer will make your web presence more useful.

Finally, as Gail Pittman, the dishware designer, points out, "Just because you build it [your web site] does not mean that people will come." Part of a comprehensive web strategy is a comprehensive plan to spread the word about your site. More about that in Chapter Seven (page 119).

The decision about where and how to sell your product is the most fundamental marketing decision you will make. But what if your product is not a tangible object but rather your time, your ideas, and your style? The next chapter takes you through some of the considerations involved in starting a service business.

Where Service Is King

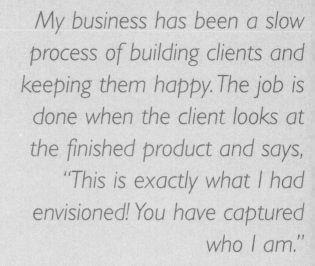

My business has been a slow process of building clients and keeping them happy. The job is done when the client looks at the finished product and says, "This is exactly what I had envisioned! You have captured who I am."

—Dawn Houser, graphic designer

Design-Based Service Businesses, Restaurants, and Inns

As essential as movers, housecleaners, plumbers, and lawyers are, this chapter is not about those kinds of service businesses. We will focus on design-oriented businesses—the kinds of service businesses that fulfill the dreams of both the owners and their clients and leave them with a profound sense of accomplishment when a job is completed. We will also say a few words about the hospitality business, including restaurants and inns. We all want more beauty in our lives. Having beautiful homes, gardens, parties, dresses, accessories, and meals are universal desires. People are willing to pay to have their environment, their looks, and their lives made more beautiful and stylish. Would you be happy to oblige them?

"Service with a smile" goes the old line, and those are not empty words. If you are thinking of starting a service business in the design field, you are more likely to succeed if spending time in close consultation with a client brings you genuine pleasure. As a design-service provider, you offer two sides of yourself to your clients: one is your talent, your style, your vision, the environment you create, or the experience you provide; the other is your ability to hear what the client wants and the flexibility to work your vision to meld with hers.

You are a great listener, a cultivator of relationships, have excellent instincts about people and you have the ability to think on your feet. Whether you are making someone's wedding gown, designing a garden, a business card, or catering a black-tie affair, you are willing to put yourself cheerfully into the service of making someone else's day/house/party/stationery/gown perfect and perfectly suited to her. For a profit of course. As Cookie Washington, the Charleston-based wedding-dress designer and maker, says, "I have to be as excited and happy about your wedding as I was about my own." She describes what she does as "catching and creating the client's vision." It's no wonder she characterizes her relationship with her clients as "symbiotic" and verging on the "psychic."

If that kind of collaboration and intimacy makes you squeamish, or the idea that what you are selling more than anything else is yourself and your time, you might want to reconsider going into the service business. Charisma and personality count for a lot in service businesses. Clients need to fall in love with you and with what you do and feel loved in return, even though, of course, you are charging them. Not for you? Perhaps a retail, manufacturing, or wholesale business is more to your liking. But for those with the right set of talents, the ability to communicate clearly—and a crystal-clear sense of billable hours—there is an ocean of opportunity in service.

The Booming Service Industry

We all value great service. We crave more service in all of our transactions: when we buy a car, fix up a house, eat a meal in a restaurant, or buy a book or an appliance. If we have the choice between two different merchants, we will go with the one that provides the best service. Service never goes out of style, and yet, sometimes it seems like such a rarity.

Because people tend to be busier than ever and many have more disposable income than in times past, they are increasingly happy to subcontract whole chunks of their lives. One reason for the boom in the service industry is that it takes care of the drudgery in our lives we no longer have time for and we can afford to pay someone else to do. We pay to have our houses cleaned and our lawns mowed, our furniture moved and our dogs walked. The service economy encompasses a wide range of human experience from the basics to the luxuries. We participate in the service economy every time we get our hair styled, hire a baby-sitter, see a doctor, or hire a consultant. No one is good at everything. Why not hire an expert to redesign a room, consult on your wardrobe, buy a gift for the boss, or help throw your daughter's birthday party?

If you are drawn to a business that enhances people's lives, gives them an experience they'll never forget, or relieves them of a burden, you are likely thinking about starting a service business.

Coming Up with an Idea for a Design-Based Service Business

Like any other business, the best service businesses stem from an entrepreneur's passion. Great restaurants are born out of a chef's passion for a particular kind of food and desire to seek the best ingredients, get in the kitchen, and create an unparalleled dining experience. The most charming and unforgettable inns arise out of someone's love for a building and its setting and the desire to decorate it, realize its potential, and share it with guests. The best dressmaker has a deep love of fabric and the knowledge that the right dress perfectly expresses and captures a woman's beauty. Garden designers have an innate love of flowers and plants. The best cake-maker wants to make the most delectable creation ever made, an edible piece of sculpture.

As with any other business, women who start design-based service businesses work incredibly hard, but because they love the materials they work with and the process of fashioning something just right for another person, and take genuine pleasure in fulfilling their clients' needs, it is labor that is truly loved. Every job is an adventure, a chance to learn and explore more about their chosen arena.

Certain kinds of service will always be with us. The hospitality industry is enormous. People will always eat in restaurants and seek out charming getaways. If your heart's desire is to open a restaurant or inn (or both) and you think you possess the peculiar set of talents to make one of these businesses work, you have your work cut out for you. Don't be intimidated out of your dream. Yes, a high percentage of restaurants fail and inns can eat up an inordinate amount of money, see seasonal fluctuations in business, go through lean times, and even go under. But the best ones, the ones that offer truly marvelous experiences to their customers that they can't get anywhere else, tend to inspire devoted followers and spawn growing circles of new ones, all the while offering a profound kind of fulfillment to their owner.

Like any other business, a good design-based service business must have a niche. The niche you decide to fill may be something you have noticed is missing from the consumer landscape. Charmaine Jones had always been interested in baking; she also had a background in art. Then she noticed there was nowhere to get fantastic, custom-designed cakes that also tasted great. "I knew there was something lacking out there and that someone should fill that gap," she says. "I decided that someone should be me. And I found my calling." What sounds like a "Eureka!" experience was actually a gradual evolution. Jones was continuing modeling clothing and baking cakes for friends on the side, when the requests for cakes began to overwhelm her. That was when the idea for her company, Isn't It Special Outrageous Cakes, was born.

If you are a born designer, you have a particular way of seeing things, a flair for putting things together. Your unique approach is, in many ways, your niche. How do you know if it is marketable? If friends are always complimenting your homemade clothes, pies, the way you put a room together, or the parties you throw, you may have the beginning of a service business. Let's face it, women, or some of them, anyway, spend a lot of time beautifying homes and gardens, fantasizing about clothes, and hosting parties, and there's no reason not to exploit your own talents in those areas if it means doing what you truly enjoy doing.

HELP WITH IMPORTANT EVENTS— ENTERTAINING

Robust industries have been built around the special events in our lives: weddings, retirements, births of our children, and birthdays. These are times when we want everything just right. It's the time to bring in the professionals to bake the cake, decorate the hall, make the perfect dress, prepare and serve a meal to our guests. If we are lucky, expense is no obstacle for these once-in-a-lifetime affairs; we are willing to pay as long as everything is perfect. Women with a strong romantic streak who enjoy making bridal fantasies come true are often drawn to wedding-related services, one of the most lucrative and personally rewarding of the design-based service businesses.

HELP WITH DESIGNING HOMES AND GARDENS

We don't always know what to do to make our homes as comfortable or stylish as possible. We have some vague ideas of the houses, rooms, and gardens of our dreams but lack the practical skills or the time to make them real. Or we have some land that we'd love to landscape and make more lovely but don't know how to begin. Having a knack for designing and decorating is, of course, a prerequisite for starting a business in beautifying people's homes. Being an interior designer or landscape designer usually requires some schooling and certification, while decorating does not.

HELP WITH DESIGNING CLOTHING AND PERSONAL ACCESSORIES

Most people want to stand out from the crowd at least sometimes, to own, wear, and cherish things that are especially made for them. Wearing a custom-made dress is an experience that can't be matched by buying something off the rack. We may want to do this once in a lifetime, say at our wedding, or a good deal more often than that. Another area where people want and need to express their individuality is with their personal or business stationery, ripe ground for graphic designers.

HELP WITH RELAXING AND ENJOYING LIFE

There are times when we just want to be pampered and served. We want to dine in a restaurant and be served food we couldn't or don't have the time or energy to make for ourselves. Or we want the perfect getaway, the B&B in the idyllic setting, with crisp sheets and antique furnishings, far away from our workaday concerns. Or we want to replenish ourselves in a spa, be treated as royalty, have our aches and wrinkles soothed away with oils and ointments straight from nature's bounty.

These are just some ideas, but these desires never go out of fashion. They pop up as sure as mushrooms in a damp climate. If you figure out how to serve people something they really want, and how to charge fairly for your time and efforts, you will never go hungry.

The Economics of a Service Business

Broadly speaking, and with some notable exceptions like restaurants, inns, and spas, service businesses are less costly to start than retail, wholesale, or manufacturing businesses. When you are primarily offering your time and expertise and don't have to stock up on materials or inventory you might not sell, overhead is usually lower, and expenses can be easily and directly transferred to the clients. Many types of service businesses offer the opportunity to start small and part-time, with just a couple of clients, and many can be operated from home.

For a design-based service business, whether it's flowers for special occasions, interior design, or custom dressmaking, you will probably need, at the very least, a camera and a professional-quality portfolio, which may cost you something to produce. You may also want to put up a web site featuring your portfolio, to give clients a preview of what you do. The portfolio, either actual or virtual, is your store, your résumé, and your catalogue rolled into one, and will go a long way in the task of selling your services. You may eventually decide that mere photographs do not do justice to your work and open a showroom, as cakemaker Charmaine Jones has, a studio, or a store to showcase your style, as floral and garden designer Rebecca Cole did when she was starting out.

In a service business, unlike a retail store, you do not need a huge inventory; you can purchase materials, whether it's fabric or flowers or flour, as clients need, and you can and should require them to pay for these materials up front. You can hire help freelance only when the workload requires. The amount of overhead depends on the nature of the business, of course. For catering or cakemaking, overhead will include some kitchen equipment and, depending on the size of the jobs you take on, rental of commercial kitchen facilities. And, unless you've got a very large home, with room for a studio, you may not last long with a home-based floral-design business.

Businesses that are fundamentally service based may also be nested in a retail business. Rebecca Cole's garden design business was headquartered in a Greenwich Village flower and garden-accessories store for its first six years. The store was in part a showcase for her style, a kind of three-dimensional portfolio. Paula Goldstein custom-mixes fragrances for clients in her store, Desana, in Boston, but she started out with a home-based, appointment-only fragrance-mixing business. The very successful high-end Manhattan interior designer Charlotte Moss also combined a retail shop with her design services.

If you do start gradually, offering your services out of your home, you'll want to conduct your home-based service business as professionally as possible. The business should have its own phone line, and consultations with clients should occur in a space that is neat, free of children's toys, interference, cooking smells, and drying laundry. Put yourself in the potential client's position. You want to inspire confidence and the feeling of being in good hands. You want the client to feel good about handing over a potentially sizable check for a third or half of the job up front.

People Skills

In a service business, unlike other kinds of businesses, you have many bosses. They are called clients. What makes service businesses unpredictable is that clients are all different. Some you will love and find to be utter joys to work with and serve; others will be mercurial, passive-aggressive, or otherwise high-maintenance and make your life a living hell. Most will lie somewhere in the middle. In a design business, which is by its nature somewhat subjective, you may encounter people who change their minds frequently and ask you to do extra work. Your native ability to read people and to ask the right questions to draw them out will prove invaluable in a service business. And your skills in this area will become more finely tuned as you go along. As with any business, your ability to learn, to adapt to new information, to avoid making the same mistake twice will determine if you sink or swim.

Your initial consultation with a client is your chance to size her up, gain her trust, and develop a rapport. You need to listen carefully. Some clients will know exactly what they want. Others will have only vague, barely articulated ideas. The latter will need your guidance and are looking for an excuse to put themselves in your hands. What sort of dress would look good on her for this special occasion? What style of cake will make her wedding spectacular? Which flowers look best in the room she wants to brighten up? Your expertise and confidence will be immensely reassuring to them. Chances are that if you are starting a business in any of these areas, you have some strong opinions and views about what looks good and what does not and a sense of the broad range of options.

When you are starting a service business, it can be hard even to think of turning a potential client away, and certainly pleasing the client is what it's all about. But there are bound to be times when you and a client are a clear mismatch. Pay attention to those little nagging intuitions about people. They usually come back to haunt you. When the service you are offering is any kind of design work, you and your client should at least share a basic aesthetic. The clients should want what you are good at making. What they want should lie somewhere in your domain of expertise. Otherwise, you're going to waste a lot of time trying to get them to like something they don't or trying to do something you are either no good at or just don't enjoy doing. "If someone wants something that we just don't do well, we refer them to someone else," says Manhattan-based garden and floral designer Rebecca Cole. "You can't bend too far over backward. You have to set your parameters and work within them."

Contracts

In any service businesses, contracts with customers are a must. These do not need to be long, abstruse legal documents chock-full of Latin phrases; they can be a two-page retainer letter or letter of agreement. But they should cover all the bases. The contract adds professionalism to your enterprise and ensures that you and the client both understand and agree on what exactly what services are to be delivered, in what time frame, and under what payment conditions. Under the best circumstances, when you and the client get along and the job goes smoothly, the contract will be signed and put in a drawer never to be consulted again. "The purpose of a contract," says Connecticut-based small-business attorney Cliff Ennico, "is to spell out what happens if you and your client disagree." According to Ennico, the following items should be covered on your contract:

1. A specific description of the services you are going to perform.

2. The amount you will be paid and what that is based on. (An hourly fee, a flat fee, a per diem fee, an hourly fee with an estimate, reimbursement for expenses, etc.)

3. When that payment is due. Is it half up front or a third now, a third halfway through, and a third on completion? Be very clear and, Ennico advises, get as much in advance as possible. Never spend money out of pocket for materials; your client should pay for those. Be very clear about the circumstances under which final payment is due, since this is generally when you make your money, with earlier payments going toward expenses incurred on the job.

4. In a design-oriented business, it may be a good idea to include a sketch or diagram of the work the client will be getting. Custom cakemaker Charmaine Jones always includes a sketch of the cake she will make for the client, making sure to get the client's approval. Floral designer Michele Rosier goes even further to ensure that she and clients are on the same page. She makes them a prototype of the arrangement they have ordered, and when they approve the prototype, usually about three weeks before before the actual event, they must pay the balance in full. Rosier says she's never had an unhappy client.

    In most design-oriented business, however, Ennico says, it's important not to guarantee the results or satisfaction on the part of the client. Satisfaction cannot be guaranteed in the highly subjective design business. This protects you from the client who may change his or her mind. (Just imagine a client who says, "You said I would love this. But I don't love this." You are not responsible for their loving it, just for delivering the services you promised to deliver, and which they agreed they wanted.)

5. Put a clause in the agreement that says that in the event of any dispute, you stop working until the dispute is resolved. Before you agree to perform any changes, write an addendum to the agreement and revise the fee, as agreed upon with your client.

Finally, have your lawyer look over the contract or agreement if you have written it yourself. At the very least, he or she may be able to point out vital aspects that may be missing in the document. To keep legal costs down, you can specify to your lawyer to spend only two or three hours on it. (See Appendix 1 on page 206 for a sample contract.)

Charging for Your Time

Although times have changed, too many women still have trouble with the notion that their time is valuable. In a service business your time (plus your vision, style, and expertise) is precisely what you are selling. Time spent can never be recouped. If you do not value the time you spend working for a client—and place a monetary value on it—then you run the risk of your clients not valuing it either.

When a client comes in with a big job, you will be faced with estimating how long it will take you to do the job. Be realistic and don't shortchange yourself. You might even add on a few hours to cover unforeseen difficulties. It may be preferable to deliver the good news that the job went more smoothly than expected and the price will actually be lower than you originally thought. Experience will eventually help you become more accurate in your time estimates.

The basis of pricing in service business is the billable hour. As its name suggests, the billable hour is the hour you can bill clients for. To determine what your hourly rate should be, figure out how many billable hours you can reasonably expect to work and carefully assess all of your costs. Then divide your total costs by your number of billable hours to get your break-even point. Inflate that to add your profit. We will delve more deeply into figuring out what your billable hour rate should be in the Pricing section in Chapter Eight.

FOLLOWING UP

Custom dressmaker Cookie Washington always makes it a point to follow up with her clients once the job is done. She strongly recommends soliciting this feedback. There may be relatively small adjustments you can make in the way you provide your services that will make clients feel even better about returning to you and recommending you to their friends. Following up is an excellent way to build rapport and loyalty and make clients feel they are important to you. It's smart marketing.

The Power of Personality in Service Businesses: Three Case Studies

❖ **REBECCA COLE**

How a floral and garden designer used a tiny retail space, books, high-profile clients, and marketing and publicity savvy to build a brand name and become a television personality.

Rebecca Cole was a transplanted country girl who, like so many young dreamers, moved to New York City to pursue an acting career. Instead, she rediscovered her love of gardening and found that her meal ticket involved designing and creating potted gardens for greenery-starved city dwellers. Curiously, her garden designing is leading her back to the entertainment business—she now has a regular stint on the *Today Show* offering gardening and lifestyle tips, a slot that a certain other entrepreneur, Martha Stewart, once filled.

Cole started on a shoestring, with a few clients who had heard of her garden design skills by word of mouth. When she decided she needed a storefront to showcase her style, she borrowed $5,000 from a wealthy client, repaying the interest in the form of garden-designing services. The tiny store, called Potted Gardens, was actually a multifaceted business, retailing flowers, botanical art, and garden antiques and serving as headquarters for her garden and floral design business. Business grew, nearly doubling every year, and she opened a second store in the tony Hamptons. Along the way, she also wrote two books extolling her ideas on garden design and giving practical tips, complete with glossy photos.

After six years of storekeeping, Cole faced a momentous business decision. She needed either to find a much bigger store or to quit retail and devote herself fully to her design business. The prohibitive commercial real estate climate in New York helped seal her decision, and she discovered she was relieved to be free of the time constraints of running a store. But the little Potted Gardens shop had done what she needed it to do. "It put us on the map and it helped get us into magazines by giving them something to shoot," says Cole.

Cole found a new space in the form of a beautiful brownstone in SoHo where she would live and work, and put a showcase garden in the back that clients would face during their consultations. Once divided evenly between retail and garden and floral design, it is now all design, and still growing. Cole has placed an $8,000 minimum on jobs, referring smaller ones to other designers, some of whom once worked for her, and sold her maintenance contracts in order to focus on designing. She is also growing her business by becoming something of a media personality, offering lifestyle hints. If it sounds like she may be nipping at the heels of Martha, it may be true.

❖ CHARMAINE JONES

How a big heart, a limitless imagination, an ability to bedazzle clients with her outrageous confections—as long as they pay the bill in full, and in advance—earned this former model the label Cake Diva.

One meeting with Charmaine Jones and you know instantly how she came by her web moniker of "Cake Diva." The former model has an outsize personality, a huge heart, and an immense talent for making cakes that almost defy description. Sometimes, they don't even look like cakes at all. Cakes made by Jones's Hoboken-based company, Isn't That Special Outrageous Cakes, may, for instance, look like the Taj Mahal, or the *Titanic*, or a fighting tank. A client once ordered an aquarium-shaped cake that featured live goldfish swimming in it. "The guests at the party had to feed the cake," Jones laughs. A great many of her cakes are for weddings— exquisite creations often with flowers so beautiful it breaks your heart to eat them. She also does cakes that are props in television shows, for soap opera weddings, and the like.

Jones knows how particular brides can be. She designed every last detail of her own wedding in a beautiful Harlem church, including her dramatic dress, the soundtrack, and, of course, the cake. What drives this artist of baking is a simple desire: "I like making people happy," she says. She not only designs and bakes a delectable cake, she delivers and, depending on how complex it is, installs it. All the client needs to do is decide what she wants, pay the bill, and, as Jones says, "take a pretty picture."

As much as her business involves creating fantasies, Jones is also a hard-nosed and realistic businesswoman. She requires payment in thirds, with the final payment one month before the wedding. "Then if the check bounces, we still have time to clear it up," she says. She is also scrupulous about creating a detailed contract that anticipates all the variables. As a veteran of modeling, she is adept at getting publicity in bridal magazines and other publications. She also has a web site, which she says has done wonders for her business. "Two-thirds of our business comes from the web," she says. "Which is good. Because then, when they come to our cake art gallery, they aren't quite as overwhelmed."

❖ COOKIE WASHINGTON

How a grown-up romantic learned to expand her horizons and her market, and capitalized on her outgoing personality to tell anyone who came within earshot about her business.

Cookie Washington of Charleston, South Carolina, sewed from the time she was seven, and grew up into what she calls a "shameless romantic" and a lover of weddings. Making a living as a designer of wedding dresses with her company Phenomenal Women was a natural career choice for her. As talented as she is as a seamstress, Washington also acknowledges that part of her success is due to her ability to connect with her clients.

After thirteen years exclusively as a wedding dress designer, Washington became inspired by one of her favorite designers, Erte, and created what she calls the "Kiss Bag." She sells this soft, formal, candy-kiss-shaped handbag, sometimes made from fabric leftover from wedding dresses, wholesale as well. Through it all, Washington has discovered that she also has a talent for marketing, which has come in handy. "I am very outgoing, and not afraid to pick up the phone and tell a writer at a newspaper or magazine about my 'Kiss Bags,'" she says. "I also successfully employed the 'three-foot rule' the first year. Anybody who got within three feet of me, I felt I had to tell about my business. People offer wonderful feedback and ideas. LISTEN!"

Her biggest mistake, she says, was in being too rigid when she first started out. "I thought because I was a plus-sized woman who knew it was nearly impossible for a woman of my size to find wedding dresses that I would design only for plus-sized women," she says. "It was years before I realized this was a big mistake. Once I started designing for women of all sizes, my business really took off." The lesson, she says, is that while you should treat your customers as you want to be treated, you should also remember that they are not all you.

Opening a Restaurant

Service is also king in the hospitality business—innkeeping and restaurants. While lots of people dream about opening a restaurant, not everyone is cut out for the business. You shouldn't even think of opening your own restaurant, says Diane Forley, owner of Verbena in New York's Gramercy Park, unless you have worked in restaurants and have a realistic sense of what running one entails. "It's very far from the glamorous photos you see in magazines," she says. Glamorous or not, with a mother who was an outstanding cook and a father who set an entrepreneurial example with his own jewelry business and had a longtime interest in all things culinary, Forley was inexorably drawn to the food business.

Certainly a love of food and the desire to create an unparalleled dining experience for people on a day-to-day basis are prerequisites for owning a restaurant. But Forley says that she spends more time on the business side of Verbena than back in the kitchen cooking. "I've had to learn accounting, budgeting, hiring, firing, staffing, customer relations, wine purchasing, publicity, being a motivator and a teacher, staying current, dealing with regulators and with maintenance, booking reservations, and imparting a philosophy," she rattles off for starters. "Then I do menu planning, teach the recipes to the cooks, and oversee dinner and lunch service."

Busy life? You bet. Forley says a typical day her first few years lasted from 8 A.M. until midnight. Along the way she has learned the importance of defining and isolating tasks and areas and delegating them. "You can't do it all yourself," she adds.

Nora Pouillon, owner of two eponymous restaurants in Washington, D.C., Restaurant Nora and Asia Nora, agrees that a successful restaurateur needs to possess enormous energy and drive as well as the ability to wear numerous hats. "You need to be creative, inventive, good with your hands, and very strong physically since you spend many hours on your feet," she begins. "You need to be a psychiatrist and a nurse. You need to hire, fire, evaluate, and be able to train people. You need to be able to convey your vision to your employees."

The vision, both women agree, comes first. For Forley, the idea was to serve seasonal and healthful food in an upscale but casual and comfortable environment. Pouillon serves seasonal and organically certified food, with a menu that changes daily, and strives for a casual but elegant ambience. But both also agree that the vision only begins to crystallize when you start looking at locations and find one that will work for you. "That's the way you begin to make it real, less of a pipe dream," says Forley. As with any other business, your location should be where your target customers can reach you. Once you have a location and a concept, says Forley, you can develop a proposal to attract investors. "I recommend not flying blind," says Forley. In other words, do plenty of research before you open a business that has the highest failure rate of any type of small business. Forley recommends talking to like-minded restaurateurs, finding mentors, and learning the formulas about such things as what a fifty-seat restaurant with an average check of $100 can expect to bring in, as well as details about how to deal with local regulators, health boards, etc. It is not the sort of information that is available in books, she cautions.

You'll need plenty of money behind you, as well as people who believe in and support you. Pouillon estimates that it takes $1 million to install a kitchen from scratch these days. Of course, you can save money if you do your own contracting or buy an existing restaurant. Karen Krasne saved money when she started Extraordinary Desserts in San Diego by buying used kitchen equipment. She started with just a few tables and gradually built her business up. In the beginning, precious resources were spent on the parts of the business that customers would see.

Over the long haul, a restaurant needs to adapt to changing times and tastes, like any other business. Kathleen Mulhern opened The Garden in Philadelphia twenty-six years ago, inspired by the al-fresco dining she enjoyed on a trip to France. At one time she did a thriving lunch business, but recent years have brought the end of the three-martini or otherwise leisurely lunch. "People are exercising and skipping lunch," she says. "Things change. You have to roll with it."

Some Restaurant-Business Missteps to Avoid

- Overstaffing; too many managers
- Poorly trained waitstaff
- Poorly laid-out kitchen
- Not enough higher-margin items like appetizers and desserts
- Bartender who does not measure
- Insufficient starting capital

An Inn of Your Own

Innkeeping is another all-encompassing job for those multi-talented people who don't mind wearing many hats. An innkeeper is chief decorator, head chef and bottle washer, hostess and handyman, salesman, and, above all, cheerfully at the disposal of her guests. To succeed in the innkeeping business, you have to love people and love serving them on a very personal level. Another aspect of life as an innkeeper is that it can be difficult for those with an intense need for privacy. This is not a nine-to-five job, and your family life may have to be woven into the fabric of your work.

Innkeeping is not the way to quick riches. But for some, it can be the perfect vocation, the ideal combination of lifestyle and life's work. Haley Eberhart and husband Bill bought the Grey Havens Inn on Georgetown Island near Bath, Maine, from Haley's mother, and they have raised their five children there. The children help out with the chores and with serving and entertaining the guests. They are part of the inn's charm. On the off-season, the family moves to Florida, and the children are home-schooled.

Some of the qualities that are indispensable if you are considering opening an inn or bed and breakfast include:

- You like meeting people
- You have a location that attracts visitors
- You like to cook and clean
- You are organized and cheerful
- You like entertaining and are hospitable by nature
- You are not afraid to deal with problems head on
- You have a sense of humor and are flexible
- You are somewhat handy
- You have a flair for creating atmosphere

Charming inns off the coast of Maine, custom dressmakers in Charleston, South Carolina, and any other business, for that matter, whether it offers a service or a product, all face a common challenge: Getting the word out with a message that is true to the business and appealing to clients and customers. The next chapter focuses on strategies to spread the word.

Getting the Word Out:
Advertising and Publicity

You'll have to appeal to your prospective customers' common sense and intelligence. Start with small, imaginative forays into promotion—small ads in a trade magazine, a hang tag on your bottle of salad dressing, simple straightforward copy on your label, or a good brochure.

—Paul Hawken, *Growing a Business*

You make something one-of-a-kind and fabulous, offer unparalleled service, have just opened a great store, or mounted a web site, but unless people know about you, your labor will have to be its own reward and your business will be short-lived. It is easy to get caught up in the day-to-day operation of your business—there's always something to do, a crisis to combat, customers to serve, suppliers to nag, staff to oversee—but marketing is what will enable you to grow. The first rule about marketing is to weave it into the fabric of every day. "For a while I had a slogan," says Leeda Marting, founder of Charleston Gardens, a fast-growing retailer of garden and home accessories, "Thirty minutes a day for marketing." That little reminder and what seemed to be a small amount of time were enough to keep Marting's mind on one of the most important aspects of growing her business.

Marketing encompasses everything you do get your products and your customers together, a large part of which is communication. But before you can communicate, you need to have something to say; before you can get the word out about your business, you need to be very clear about what its main message, image, and selling points are. These should be embedded in your business plan and stated in succinct language as a guide, reminder, and framework for everyone involved in your company.

Once you are clear about your message, you will need to develop and constantly refine your strategies for reaching the right people with it. A well-chosen location and a good sign are just a start. Targeting the right people and giving them an effective message that will measurably increase your sales without spending too much money will draw on all of your native communication skills, savvy, and ingenuity.

Reaching out to potential customers through promotion, advertising, and public relations can be the first step in establishing a relationship, one that ideally will be ongoing. Like every other part of your business, your efforts to publicize, promote, and market it are an expression of the kind of businesswoman you are. Everything from clever copy on a hang tag to a small but elegant ad in a trade publication should be part of a coherent whole that honestly communicates to your customer the kind of product or service they can expect from you.

The Importance of Word of Mouth

As important as advertising and publicity are, there is no substitute for good word of mouth. Without it, success is likely to elude even businesses that spend millions on promotion and advertising. And there's no bigger black mark than bad word of mouth. If the people who actually buy things from you are not satisfied, fail to recommend you to their friends, or, worse, steer them away, you will be fighting an uphill battle to overcome the bad reviews for a long time to come.

If you are going to rely heavily on word of mouth, it may be worth remembering that the words out of some mouths carry more weight than the words out of others. Cookie Washington's wedding-dress and soft-accessories business has been greatly helped by a friendship she has struck up with plus-sized actress Camryn Mannheim. Likewise, actress Helen Hunt's support for Michele Rosier's flower business, Flowers by Michele in Santa Monica, has proved invaluable. The public may be more inclined to listen to popular or local celebrities, so use any connection you can to reach people with influence.

Or you may want to strategically target people who have influence within your industry. The Swedish-born makeup company, FACE Stockholm took the rather ingenious marketing approach of ensuring that makeup artists in the fashion and beauty industry were equipped with FACE Stockholm products in their kits. These influential people then helped spread the word that FACE Stockholm was a must-have for those interested in fashion and beauty. The upstart makeup company's name also frequently appeared in the credits of fashion spreads.

While word of mouth is vital, it is a rare business that grows by virtue of word of mouth alone, and few entrepreneurs can afford to take an entirely laissez-faire approach to marketing. To jump-start your thinking about how to spread the word about your business, make it a point to notice what kinds of marketing techniques work for you as a customer. Whose word do you rely on? How do you find out about the things you buy? Are there ads that catch your attention and make you curious? Cut them out or take note of them. Are there articles or publications you read for the purpose of learning where you can find an item? Study those publications and acquaint yourself with the writers who cover your industry. Analyze their approach, their angle, and their style. You may want to pitch stories about your company to them. How do other businesses in your industry and businesses you admire spread the word? Can you adapt that technique to your business?

Promoting Your Business

An opening party, a booth at a street fair, free samples of your product, small giveaway items like mugs, hats or T-shirts, and sponsorship of charitable causes and events are all promotional activities that can create awareness and goodwill about your business. You should try to work a few of these activities into your plans from the outset.

PARTIES

For stores, an opening party or grand-opening event provides an excellent introduction to the neighborhood and serves to make a wider group of people aware and interested enough to come back, browse, and buy. They are also likely to tell their friends about the beautiful shop they visited and some of the items they saw for sale there. To make an opening party even more memorable, consider giving your guests small goodie bags.

You don't have to spend a fortune to throw a party. Be resourceful about ways you can save money, perhaps by bartering with other local businesses. Throwing a party does require some effort, of course. Little touches like homemade food are always appreciated. Invite the press. Reporters love free food and other treats as much as anyone else, and, at the very least, the local newspaper should write a short piece about a new business in town.

Tracy and John Porter threw a memorable party when they opened their store, Stonehouse Farm Goods, a showcase for Tracy's designs, in Princeton, Wisconsin. "When we opened our store, our goal was to create a grand-opening experience in our own environment that would be unforgettable," Tracy recounts. "Cocktails were served. A lovely feast was provided, with plenty of dessert, of course. As a way to mark the evening, we made a toast, and each guest opened a tiny gift box they had received earlier in the evening and more than a hundred butterflies were released in the store."

Some businesses host regular parties as an important part of their marketing strategy. Holiday parties are always popular. They can boost holiday sales or move items in the off-season. Invite your regular customers and encourage them to bring friends. Marsha and Roger Alldis, the husband and wife who own Tancredi & Morgan in Carmel, California, throw two or three theme parties a year, inviting their entire mailing list. Several hundred people usually attend. Not only do the Alldises' love dreaming up ideas for and hosting parties, the practice has directly benefited sales at the eclectic antiques, clothing, and herbs store.

SAMPLING

Another promotional strategy that has served some businesses extremely well is distributing free samples, both to the public at large and to press and other influential people in the trade. If you make something that can be broken down into small packages and are convinced it will sell itself once people try it, sampling can be the way to go. This is the logic behind your favorite bakery offering free nibbles of carrot cake at the counter, the ice cream store offering a dab of a new flavor on a small wooden spoon, or someone roaming around the supermarket offering shoppers cubes of cheese. Tiny bottles of mouthwash that arrive in your mailbox and packets of moisturizer glued to magazine pages are also attempts to spread the word through sampling. This approach can be extremely successful for a small business. The mom-and-pop beauty and skin products business Kiehl's sampled their way into the mass market.

Samples can be offered on a variety of scales. You may want to send samples just to press people and others who are influential in your industry. Christine Dimmick, founder of the Good Home Company, which makes bath and beauty potions, employs this technique every time she develops a new product. "I send samples and a cover letter to the beauty editors at the appropriate magazines," she says. "You don't have to buy a list. You just look at the masthead."

Another way to go is to enter samples of your product in a contest. Fredericksburg Herb Farm frequently uses this sampling tack with their homemade herbal products. When the owners, Sylvia and Bill Varney, submitted their edible flowers herb vinegar to the National Association for the Specialty Food Trade and won an award, their business took flight and they were hard-pressed to fill all of the wholesale orders.

When she was starting out, Santa Monica–based floral designer and arranger Michele Rosier made arrangements out of two-day-old, no longer sellable flowers and gave them to people in the neighborhood. "All I asked was that they return the vase," she said. The technique was extremely successful, bringing people into her shop, giving them a sense of her style, and getting them interested in Flowers by Michele. How did she think of it? "You get very creative when you're desperate," she says.

MUTUAL BENEFITS

What can be better than doing well while doing good? Charitable involvement is and should be its own reward, but it can also be great public relations for your business. Sponsoring an event like a walk for breast cancer or the local softball team are win-win situations, so don't shy away from opportunities like these. The relationship between your business and the community it serves is symbiotic, and when people perceive you not only as a quality purveyor but as a good citizen, your stock will rise in their eyes. Solid involvement in the community will also improve your profile in bankers' eyes. Donations from your business to charity need not amount to a lot, and the benefits far outweigh the expense. Restaurants can give food to homeless shelters, floral designers can donate flower arrangements for senior citizens' homes. Craftspeople can donate wares for benefit auctions. Whether your gift is high or low profile, it's good for the soul, and potentially good for the bottom line.

Pittsburgh antiques dealer Marlene Harris virtually launched her business when she donated a piece of antique porcelain-button jewelry to a charity auction, in part to see what price it would fetch. A buyer from a local department store happened to be in attendance, and while the charity was helped, the two struck a deal that turned into a seventeen-year relationship.

When she opened her first Wicker Garden store in Manhattan, Pam Scurry threw a Halloween party for the children in the neighborhood as a gesture of goodwill. It did not hurt her business when the local press labeled her the "Good Witch of the Upper East Side" as a result. Naturally, the publicity translated into more business.

When you first open your business, especially a store, you will probably be inundated with requests for sponsorships and your participation in local charitable activities. Of course, you won't be able to help everyone out and will have to learn to say no, even though it can be painful. You must decide which causes are most important to you and make the most sense in terms of your business. The trick also is not to be too cynically calculating in your forays into charity. If people perceive that you are doing good merely for the sake of good publicity, they are apt to tune out those efforts.

The Printed Word

We may live in a digital age, but the printed word in all of its myriad forms still exerts a powerful influence in the marketplace. For starters, your sign, calling card, hang tags, and shopping bags are all marketing tools. That is, they are opportunities to get your business's name and style out into the world and into your customers' minds and to communicate a message about who you are. Take the time to come up with the right design for your logo first. Your logo is an important symbol for your business and a way for customers to recognize you and your products instantly. If graphic design is not your forte, hire someone to help design and develop your logo, and to figure out how to incorporate it thematically into your business's stationery supplies, such as letterhead, business cards, packaging, bags and labels.

After your logo, your business card is probably the next most important graphic design project, and an item you will want to disseminate liberally. Even within the somewhat narrow parameters of business cards, you need to find a way to express your business's unique style. Typeface, color, paper stock, and slight variations in the card's overall shape and size are all elements you can play with. (If you want to get an idea of how creative and evocative calling cards can be, look at *Victoria*'s book on the subject: *Calling Cards: Business and Calling Card Design*.)

Finally, what kind of a package will customers carry with them when they leave your store or business? If you can come up with some clever kind of package, it's a perk that may help sway customers to return and to tell their friends, or it might be seen by others, pique their curiosity, and spur them to stop by. When Leslie Ross first started The Thymes Limited, the Minneapolis-based bath, body care, and home fragrance business, she garnered nearly as much attention and delight for her clever packaging—some products were packed in Chinese food takeout containers, for instance—as she did for her products.

BROCHURES, FLIERS, NEWSLETTERS, AND DIRECT MAIL

After you have your needed stationery and packaging supplies, it is a good idea to generate other forms of literature about your business to give or to send to prospective customers. Sometimes referred to as "marketing collateral," these items include brochures, fliers, and newsletters. This type of literature need not be expensive to produce, but it should be visually appealing, easy to read, and should spark potential customers' curiosity and interest. Whenever you print literature about your business, be sure to include information about where to contact and find you. If you can write catchy and informative copy about your products, how they will benefit customers, and what's new with your business that customers might be interested in, you'll be ahead of the game.

Or, if not writing, you may have other talents you can utilize. Potter Karen Skelton used her photography skills to create colorful postcards of her ceramic creations to help spread the word—and the image—of her business, Potluck Studios in Accord, New York. Obviously, when it comes to beautiful objects, pictures can be worth more than the pithiest words. For other kinds of products and businesses, you may want to consider illustration as the visual component in your brochures or catalogues. Illustration conveys an upscale feeling to a business's literature.

Don't despair if you are not a writer, graphic artist, or photographer. Your biggest asset in your business is your genuine feeling for your product and your customers. Your customers are, after all, a version of you; *you* should want to receive your services or product. The best kind of communication, no matter what the media, is honest, direct, heartfelt, and true.

Brochures, fliers, newsletters, and catalogues are all tools you can use in a direct-mail campaign, which is an extremely targeted method for getting your message out, since you can select the people receiving it. Maintaining and building a good mailing list is vital for these efforts. In some cases, such as when you are trying to expand, you may want to purchase a list from a list-broker. If this is too expensive, you may want to consider bartering for a list from a noncompeting business in your neighborhood that might cater to the same demographic group. Whether you buy or barter the list, choose it carefully. Make sure it is targeted to the people who are likely to be interested in your product or service. You do not want to waste time and money on people who are likely to see your brochure or flier as junk mail. (See Chapter Five for tips on building and maintaining a mailing list.)

Direct mail is an opportunity to build your relationship with your customer, and it can be extremely effective. Direct mail is advertising and sales wrapped up in one printed piece. When writing a direct-mail piece, whether it is a catalogue, flier, or brochure, use a friendly and personal writing style, as if you were having a conversation with the person or writing them a letter. Focus on the benefits to the customer that your product or service offers. Offer something for a limited time and include a call to action. One way to break through the clutter of junk mail people receive and make your package more intriguing to them, is to make your package three-dimensional, by adding a tiny sample or other lightweight object inside.

Keeping in Touch with Your Customers

It is smart business to keep and maintain a mailing list of interested customers so you can send notices about sales, specials, or new items or services you're offering through the mail. This kind of target marketing, where you reach select prospects in the comfort of their home, is called direct marketing. But these days, you might also consider keeping in touch with your customers via e-mail and direct e-marketing. It's cheaper than the postal service, more interactive, and many people find it to be an extremely convenient mode of communication. Though too much junk e-mail is liable to annoy people as much as old fashioned junk mail, carefully planned e-marketing can be effective.

Electronic communication goes both ways, of course, and you should consider encouraging your customers to contact you by e-mail as well. It has the advantage of being less disruptive to you than the telephone—you can read and respond to e-mail at your convenience. (You should broadcast your e-mail address, as well as your web site if you have one, on all of your company's literature, press releases, business cards, etc., much as you would a phone number.) Invite feedback and communication from your customers , and offer to deliver them information via e-mail. Try to respond to e-mails from customers promptly, within a day or two. Keep an e-mail database much as you would a mailing list, and send follow-up e-mails when someone purchases something from you as well as holiday greetings.

Publicity—Public or Press Relations

Apart from promotional activities, the two other ways of getting the word out about your business are publicity and advertising. Each has its place. But publicity—also known as PR, press relations, and public relations—has some distinct advantages. It's free, or nearly free, so even if it does not get great results, you haven't lost anything except a little time, whereas advertising can be quite costly and still not get you any results. Publicity gives credibility to your business, since the implication is that the editors, or writers, of the magazines or newspapers or TV shows are at least tacitly endorsing your product or business by mentioning it (assuming that they are mentioning it favorably).

Publicity does have one disadvantage, however, which is that you have less control over the message than you do when you purchase advertising. At most publications, the good ones anyway, the editors control the message, and some will bristle at any implication that they should toot your horn in exactly the way you want it tooted. To get mentioned in a magazine or a newspaper, or on a television show, you will need to fit into their overall vision, so you need to study them before you approach them.

So if publicity is free and advertising is costly, why don't budget-minded businesspeople just choose publicity as a way of getting the word out? Probably because they are intimidated and don't quite understand how one goes about getting publicity. We'll let you in on a little secret: Editors of magazines and other publications and producers of television magazines and talk shows need content and stories to fill their pages, and they can't come up with that content in a vacuum. In short, they won't know about you if nobody tells them. You may even be doing them a favor by sending them information about your company, along with beautiful pictures of your new product. This does not mean that they need you as much as you need them. After all, lots of other businesses are competing for their attention. But there are things you can do to increase your chances of getting some coverage. "You have to let them know that you have something that is worth their time," says Leeda Marting, who has been extremely successful in getting publicity for Charleston Gardens in gardening and home magazines. "I try to think like the writer. I ask myself, What can I give them that will make it easier for them to write their story? Then I try to give it to them before they ask."

HOW TO GET PUBLICITY

For starters, do your research. Read as much as possible material that is pertinent to your field. Read trade magazines, consumer magazines, and newspapers that are relevant. Do they run regular columns or features about a business like yours? Make a note if a particular TV show airs stories like the one you want to tell. Zero in on writers who cover the industry you are in, with whom you have a shared interest. What angle do they take? What's their style? What seems to interest them? Reporters and editors are busy people and they receive hundreds of pitches weekly. The ones that are off base are quickly jettisoned or filed in the circular file.

Build a list of media contacts, otherwise known as a press list, with names, phone and fax numbers, e-mail, and snail-mail addresses. Make sure you spell everyone's name correctly, and keep up with their title changes. Don't send material to the editor-in-chief; choose the appropriate department—the beauty editor, fashion editor, or food editor, for example. When the opportunity presents itself, try to meet reporters at trade shows and industry functions. Cultivate relationships with a few writers and editors. The successful Manhattan interior designer Charlotte Moss went a step further when she started her business. She invited the editors of magazines she wanted to appear in to tea, one at a time. That made each editor feel special and privy to inside information. Reporters and editors want stories that are exclusive. They do not want to feel like one of the pack. It will not be a selling point if your story has already been run by their closest competitor.

Understanding how reporters and writers work will increase your chances of approaching them at the right time and getting them interested in you. First and foremost, reporters and editors work under deadline pressure, and they can be grumpy and brusque if you interrupt the process of making a deadline. Daily newspapers, of course, have daily deadlines, usually in the afternoon, so it's better to call in the morning. When you call an editor or writer at any publication, it is a good idea to ask first whether they are on deadline or if they have time to talk. Based on the information you glean, make a note on your media database about what times are good to contact the writers you have chosen.

Lead time is also an important factor when it comes to print publications. For instance, monthly magazines are generally written, edited, and closed at least three months in advance of the publication date. If you want to be included in a Christmas shopping issue, they need the information in July or August. Got a gift that would be perfect for Mother's Day? Send out the pictures and press releases to the monthlies in January or February. If the publication is weekly, plan to send your press release three to six weeks in advance of when you'd like to see it published. One week early is a good rule of thumb for newspapers.

When you do get a reporter/writer or editor on the phone, don't be vague and chatty. It helps if you can put your business, your story, into some kind of current context, like a trend. If you are insightful and quotable and to the point, the reporter may even call you for a quote in a relevant story in the future, which gives you another chance to plug your business. If a reporter ever does call you, be sure to return the call promptly, again because of deadlines. You wouldn't want them to call and quote your competitor instead.

Finally, if a reporter is brusque or seems to brush you off, don't take it personally. Most likely it has to do with job pressures, and nothing to do with you.

PRESS KITS, PRESS RELEASES

For your dealings with the media, you'll need to have a press kit. This is a kind of one-stop shop for reporters, a handy pocket folder containing all the information they need to write a story about you or to include you in a larger story. Press kits, or media kits, range from relatively simple and modestly produced to expensive and slick, depending on your budget. Commonly, they are pocket folders with the following items inside:

- one-page background on your company

- business card

- press release announcing your big news—the story you hope they'll write (more on this below)

- photographs—many publications may use your photographs rather than take their own

- reprints of any articles that have appeared about your company or you

- company profile and fact sheets

- biographies of principals

- brochures, catalogues, or other business literature

You don't have to send the entire press kit every time. Use your judgment and don't waste effort and postage. Publications receive many of these, and many are thrown out. You may want to wait until a writer or editor asks for more information because she plans to do a story. Sometimes, just faxing or e-mailing the press release or background information is all that is needed.

A press release is written in the style of a news story, which means that it should use the classic journalistic format of an inverted pyramid; that is, you should begin with the big news and include all the vital information—who, where, when, and perhaps how and why. Then you follow with more details and context for the big news. The reason for the inverted pyramid is so that even if someone stops reading before the end, they will still get the vital information you want to convey. If your press release is well written, concise, and appropriate, some publications will print it as is. Be brief and factual, and use clear, simple language. Avoid jargon, hype, and adjectives. Make sure you check for typos, and always tell reporters where they can get more information. One page, two at the most, should suffice. (See Appendices 2 and 3 on pages 208 and 209 for sample press releases.)

BECOME AN EXPERT

The surest way to be considered an expert in your industry is to write a book. Helen Cox, of As You Like It Silver Shop, found that out when she wrote a book about silver patterns. Rebecca Cole has written gardening books. Rachel Ashwell, of Shabby Chic, has several decorating books out. Not only is writing a book an excellent way to be dubbed an expert, it is an excellent exercise in brand extension.

But if you are not quite ready to write your own tome, some entrepreneurs do speaking engagements and others write how-to articles for appropriate trade journals. These efforts are less of a commitment than a book and can help spark interest in both your business and in you. Of course, it helps if you genuinely enjoy these activities. Debby DuBay, owner of Limoges Antiques in Andover, Massachusetts, is active in her local Historic Society and frequently accepts invitations to speak about her passion, Limoges china. Manhattan-based antique jewelry dealer Camilla Bergeron speaks frequently to audiences expressing her views on her favorite subject. Christine Dimmick offers advice about homemade beauty products and lifestyle on the web.

If you become known to reporters and editors as something of an expert in your industry, and a quotable and reliable source, chances are they'll put you in their Rolodex and call you up for comment when they are writing a story that's relevant. If so, get over any mistrust you may harbor about the media and comply with these requests. Being an expert source is great publicity and it costs you nothing. Return reporters calls promptly, and give them quality information that is not just blatant hype about your business.

Advertising

Advertising is probably the most obvious way to get your message out. It is also the costliest, which can make it prohibitive to many start-up and small businesses except if done on a very small scale. Still though, advertising has its advantages, and if you choose your outlets carefully, it can serve an important purpose in growing your business. The advantage of advertising is that in exchange for money, you have total control over your message, unlike with publicity or editorial.

The challenge to the business owner when it comes to advertising is twofold:

1. Creating a good and effective ad that communicates what you want to communicate. Advertising should both create awareness about your business, and inspire people to seek you out.

2. Choosing the right medium for your message. Whether newspaper, magazine, cable-TV station, web site, or radio station, the right medium is the one that reaches the people you want to reach (your target market) or the people you think will be interested in buying what you sell.

When you advertise, most experts recommend that you set definite goals. Some questions to ask yourself are: What market do I want to reach? What image do I want to convey? Which product or service do I want to promote? A good ad creates awareness and inspires action. It needs to convey not only basic information like who, what, when, where, why, and possibly how much, but also a message telling how your business, product, or service will make somebody's life better.

As a new business, you will probably be inundated with pitches to advertise in various publications and venues, and some advertising salespeople will be extremely aggressive in their efforts to convince you that your success rides on advertising with them. Advertising can eat up a lot of money for negligible returns, so you need to be extremely selective and be able to cut through the sales pitches.

A good part of what will inform your advertising decisions will be your budget. One rule of thumb is that your advertising budget should be between 2 and 10 percent of your estimated yearly gross. Unless you are extremely well funded you won't be able to afford large ads in glossy national magazines.

There are advantages and disadvantages to just about every medium, which you should keep in mind when deciding where to advertise and designing or producing your ad. Local newspapers, for instance, reach people in a given area, although they are not that targeted otherwise, and advertising space in them is relatively inexpensive. But newspapers have no shelf life, and photographs don't reproduce well in them. Other relatively inexpensive advertising venues include local radio or cable-TV spots and small ads in trade magazines. You may also want to explore advertising on the World Wide Web, such as banner ads on sites you think your potential customers are apt to visit, though banner ads are not widely recognized as being an effective advertising medium yet.

Wherever you advertise, keep careful track of which ads and venues seem to generate responses to your business. Always ask new customers how they found out about you and make a note of what works best. As with anything else in business, making mistakes is not as bad as failing to learn from them.

Hiring the Experts

If you have a big enough budget, you may want to consider hiring a publicist or advertising agency. Apart from benefiting from a publicist's expertise, it can be more comfortable to let someone else talk you up to reporters. But this is not a task you can farm out entirely, and the cost can be prohibitive for a start-up. You will first need to do your research and make sure that the agency or person you are hiring knows your industry and which media outlets to target. Publicists get paid no matter what kind of results they get for you, so hiring the wrong one can be an expensive mistake. Find out who else they represent and what kind of relationships they have with important editors. You will also need to work closely with whomever you hire to make sure the strategy fits with your overall vision and business goals.

Hiring the wrong publicist can prove to be an expensive and fatal error. Manhattan-based antique-jewelry dealer Camilla Bergeron says she has seen businesses like hers fail when they hired publicists more

MY ADVICE ON ADVERTISING

ISABEL GARRETON, clothing designer, Palos Verdes, California

Advertisement is more effective after you have started and learned enough through success and failures about what works and what doesn't. It is easier to respond then to a larger demand, which is what advertisement will bring. Focus your advertisement on your targeted client. For example, if you sell communion dresses, advertise in local Catholic school and church publications, at their festivals and school plays, or volunteer to sponsor their sports team. Work within your budget.

How I Spread the Word

HELEN COX,
As You Like It Silver Shop,
New Orleans

When I first started out I had to rely on an occasional classified ad and word of mouth. A couple of writers for local publications did stories on this unique business (there are very few shops around the country that specialize in sterling silver). Having a booth at antique shows was a wonderful way to advertise—the shows increased my business tremendously.

Now we run ads in several tourist publications aimed at the socioeconomic group interested in our product. We also have a pretty brochure showing the kinds of things we have in stock. We donate to silent auctions around town, which raise funds for charitable causes. In 1994, I published a 130-page book entitled Silver Flatware: An Illustrated Guide to Pieces, Manufacturers and Care. *Authoring a book makes you an instant expert. Speaking engagements and a lot of free advertising resulted. I sent copies to many magazines hoping to stir some interest and that resulted in a wonderful article in* Victoria *magazine. Also, there was a nice article in* Southern Accents *and a review in* Silver Magazine, *a trade publication.*

interested in getting write-ups in the society pages than in the fashion magazines. "You want a publicist who really knows the business," says Bergeron. "A real working publicist, not just one with a high-society name."

The bottom line is that no one knows your product/service/store better than you, and no one else has as much stake in promoting it effectively and honestly. More than a few successful entrepreneurs will steer you away from spending your much-needed start-up capital on these consultants. (For more on hiring a publicist, see Chapter Nine.)

Keeping the Numbers:
Financial Management

CHAPTER EIGHT

*Make it a point to do
something every day that you
don't want to do. This is
the golden rule for acquiring
the habit of doing your
duty without pain.*

—Mark Twain

There is no escaping the fact that business involves numbers and record-keeping and making sure that everything not only adds up but adds up to a profit as well as a positive cash flow. Even with the best-laid plans and scrupulous records, plenty of bends in the road and surprises will keep the entrepreneurial adventure interesting. The stress and potential costs of not being on top of the numbers, not keeping good records, letting paperwork pile up into unmanageable chaos, and not being able to find information when you need it, or when the IRS needs it, are just not worth it. Such worries will take you away from the more creative aspects of running your business. Poor recordkeeping, pricing that fails to take all the factors and costs into account, and other kinds of financial mismanagement are among the most commonly cited mistakes new businesses make and are frequent causes of their demise.

You don't have to be a whiz at numbers to understand that a business makes money when its income exceeds its expenses. But figuring out how to make that happen is a bigger challenge than many business owners realize. For starters, you need to know the kinds of numbers that are standard in your industry, which you can research through trade associations and publications. Try to get a good idea of what kinds of ratios between sales and expenses you need to aim for. Get a handle on what percentage of your income can be spent on things like labor, rent, and advertising, so that you can make sure to price things so that your business can turn a profit. You need to know how many sales you have to make to break even; if you are charging by the hour, you need to calculate how many hours you can reasonably work and charge for. You need to calculate your break-even point, and then you need to keep roughly on course toward reaching those targets.

You may develop your own system of recordkeeping, one that peculiarly suits your business and your style. But there are certain standardized methods and forms that all businesses use and should follow. Every business needs a ledger of daily activities, a chart of accounts, annual balance sheets, monthly income statements, and weekly or monthly cash-flow statements. These accounting fundamentals will be explained in this chapter.

Certainly, you need a good accountant to guide and advise you and help you plan your business, and most businesses also employ at least a part-time bookkeeper as well, but don't allow yourself to be murky about the financial realities of conducting your business. You should generally have a good sense of where you stand at all times. You should know how much cash you have, how much is coming in, what you owe, and what you are owed.

Pricing Basics and Strategies

Deciding what to charge for your products or service ranks among the the most important business decisions. In fact, a poor pricing strategy, or "emotional pricing" as it is sometimes known, is one of the most common causes of business failure. To avoid it, take pen to paper and get ready to calculate costs, markups, and profit expectations. Pricing may not be an exact science, and you may find yourself adjusting your prices from time to time, but that does not mean it should be complete guesswork.

Obviously, pricing affects how much money you make or lose. It also affects your market, how your product is perceived, who will buy from you, how they feel about the transaction, and whether they come back for more. Most customers want to feel either that they got a good deal or that they received something of great value. As a merchant, you can be the cheapest or you can be the best, but probably not both. You have to decide which it will be. Business is at its best, after all, when both customer and merchant get something they wanted on terms they like.

There are two ways of approaching pricing:

1. *Cost-based*, which is basing the price of an item on how much it cost you to produce or bring to the market.

2. *Value-based*, which relates to how valuable the item is to your customer, regardless of its cost to you.

You need to incorporate both approaches in your pricing decisions. If you charged customers exactly what an item cost you, you would merely break even. So the cost to you is the minimum price to the customer. On the other end of the spectrum, the maximum is how much the customer is willing to pay, or how valuable it is to him or her. This is known as pricing according to "what the market will bear." The fair price is somewhere in the middle.

COST-BASED PRICING

It might seem simple, but cost-based pricing is much more complicated than making sure you charge more than what you paid for a given item. Even figuring out what your costs are is trickier than you might think, because there are two kinds of costs, direct and indirect. For retailers, for instance, the cost of a product is not exactly what was paid for it at a trade show or on a buying trip. That's merely the direct cost. You might think that if you paid

$10 for something, then charged your customers $20 you have profited by $10, but you have not factored in all the expenses, such as travel costs and freight. "Spend a lot of time figuring out exactly what it costs to bring a product to market," advises Leeda Marting, founder and owner of Charleston Gardens. "The product costs more than just what you paid the manufacturer."

Figuring out the direct costs incurred to produce an item is not that difficult. The trick is also taking indirect costs, also known as overhead, into account. In other words, you need to have a firm idea of the total costs of running your business before you can price for profit. That includes rent, insurance, administrative costs, utilities, licenses, and the interest on that loan you took out. These are bills that must be paid regardless of how much business you are doing. At Fredericksburg Herb Farm, for example, which is a multifaceted business, pricing is an extremely complicated affair. Among other fixed costs is the nearly $1,000 a month the company pays for liability insurance, which needs to be factored into prices, says Bill Varney, co-owner with his wife, Sylvia.

If you are paying sales people, then their salaries are part of your cost of sales. If you are selling by catalogue, the costs of printing and mailing catalogues are part of your cost of sales. These costs must be covered with your sales, or you won't make money. "When you cost out your product, you have to take into account your materials, cost of production, administrative expenses, and selling expenses," says Mary Ella Gabler, owner of Peacock Alley, a supplier of bed and bath luxury linens. So be extremely thorough when you sit down to figure out the total cost of running your business.

Types of Costs

Direct costs (also known as variable expenses, costs of goods sold, jobsite expenses): These vary with volume, and, as the name suggests, are directly related to the item sold.

Indirect costs (also known as overhead, fixed costs): These include rent, storage, equipment, insurance, utilities, interest, administrative salaries, etc. These are bills you have to pay no matter how much business you are doing.

From an analysis of your costs, you can figure out your cost per unit. From that, you can figure out your break-even point, the amount you need to charge per item or per hour just to recoup all of your costs, not to make any profit. That amount is your minimum price. You should dip below that only temporarily and for a specific reason, to gain market share, say, or possibly to generate some quick cash flow.

The hard part of analyzing your costs is in breaking down the indirect, or fixed, costs and figuring out what portion of them should be paid for by each job or item. This computation can be quite involved, and some of it is educated guesswork, to be sure. Obviously, one sale or one customer does not pay your entire month's rent. You and your accountant or other financial advisers should be able to come up with a percentage of your markup, or a percentage of your hourly rate if yours is a service business, that goes toward overhead. You also need to have a good handle on the kind of volume you must do in order to cover your costs and make a profit.

Seamstress Cookie Washington worked in consultation with her accountant to come up with a pricing strategy that makes sense for her business. Her overhead is relatively low, since she works out of a studio in her Charleston home. Still, her business needs to cover the appropriate portion of her mortgage, about a third, as well as a salary for her. Cookie's hourly rate is $35, and out of that she figures about $10 goes toward overhead, leaving her with $25 per hour in wages.

VALUE-BASED PRICING

Value-based pricing is more subjective than cost-based pricing, and figuring it out does not involve crunching a lot of numbers. It involves assessing the marketplace. Value-based pricing requires you to perform that all-important exercise of thinking like a customer. How much are people willing to pay for your product and why? What benefits does your product or service offer customers? How can you make your product more valuable in their eyes. Your reputation, packaging, sales environment, and level of service all contribute toward increasing the perceived value of your product, as do some other even less-tangible factors. If your product has cachet and is unique, like a piece of art, a one-of-a-kind piece of clothing, or a collector's item, you can charge even more for it. The act of imbuing your product with value and mystique unrelated to its actual cost is another aspect of marketing.

To zero in on the value of your goods or services to customers, find out what the competition is charging for similar items and acquaint yourself with your industry's standards. Dinnerware designer Gail Pittman puts it succinctly: "Pricing is what the market will bear for what you deliver." Obviously if what the market will bear does not cover your costs, you've got a problem.

You should always be on the alert for people's reactions to your wares and their prices. When seamstress and clothing designer Cookie Washington first introduced her "Kiss Bag," she asked certain trusted clients what they would be willing to pay for such an item. Christine Dimmick, of the Good Home Company, says she takes careful note of how clients react to her prices. "If they say, 'Oh, that's so reasonable,' then I know that I might be able to jack it up a little," she says.

When you are selling something that is similar to what others sell, your price needs to be similar to theirs, within a dollar or so, otherwise it may appear that you are price-gouging. No one likes to learn that they paid a lot of money for an item they could have bought much more cheaply. And some will do their research in advance, and buy where they get the best deal, which will cost you their business.

HOW I APPROACH PRICING

CHARMAINE JONES, Isn't That Special Outrageous Cakes, Hoboken, New Jersey

I figured out what other people are charging for specialty cakes and how much it cost me in labor and materials. Then I found a happy medium. The important thing is making the client happy, but not giving it away, like you're somebody's grandmother. If you don't charge enough, people will think there's something wrong with it. They'll think you don't value it, so why should they?

PRICING LUXURY AND ONE-OF-A-KIND ITEMS

If you make or sell something that is one of a kind or custom-make an item, as Jones does, you have a little more leeway on pricing. For one thing, you can position your product as totally unique, the best in the industry, a "prestige" product, and charge a lot for it. For luxury items, targeted to affluent customers, a high price can be part of the mystique. (Think Rolex watches.) If everyone could afford to own this item, the appeal might be lost.

Keep in mind, however, that setting a price near the top of what the market will bear also carries certain expectations you must be prepared to deliver on. People who are willing to pay top dollar want the extras: extra service, personal attention, unquestioned willingness to take returns, make refunds, or make alterations.

SERVICE-BUSINESS PRICING AND BILLABLE HOURS

Service providers are paid for their time, so fundamental to their pricing equation is the notion of billable hours. Billable hours are hours for which you can bill customers. The first step is figuring out how many hours you can reasonably expect to work directly for clients, without running yourself into an early grave or neglecting the other aspects of running your business. It might be reasonable to estimate that you can devote roughly four hours per eight-hour day to direct client service, thus twenty hours per week, a thousand hours per year (leaving two weeks for vacation). The other four hours a day are left for administrative tasks, paperwork, marketing, sweeping the floor, and whatever else is needed to run your business.

Next you need to figure out all of the costs associated with running your business. That means all costs, direct and indirect. To get your break-even price, divide your total costs per year by your billable hours per year. If you charge that amount you'll neither lose nor make money. Any higher than that, and you are operating at a profit; lower, and you're operating at a loss. Even though you have figured out your price based on billable hours, this doesn't mean you have to bill your clients by the hour. You just need to incorporate this knowledge into your overall fees for jobs.

Though you may be tempted to establish your price based on the going rate or what others in your industry are charging, do make a point of figuring out your costs to make sure that you are covering them. If you discover that you have to charge a lot more than you thought to break even, then make a concerted attempt to position yourself as a business offering something that is not to be found elsewhere in the marketplace.

MARKUP AND MARGINS

A common way of setting a price is to multiply the cost times a certain percentage, also called your markup. The percentage difference between the cost to you and the price the customer pays is your margin of profit. So your profit margin is directly related to your markup rate.

ADVICE ON PRICING FROM ENTREPRENEURS

Don't give out a quote too quickly. Digest it. Tell the client you'll think it through. Figure out the cost of the materials and how long it will take you to make the item. Then add extra. Remember, there's a point where people won't pay any more for an item.

—Joyce Ames, custom lampshade designer
and maker, New York

I price by the piece and then I charge a setup fee. When you first start out, you don't know how long things are going to take, but with experience you'll get better at estimating. I mark up by as much as three and four times. The exception is if I'm doing a big event where there will be lots of press and good publicity; if I risk losing the job by charging a lot, then I might lower my price.

—Michele Rosier, Flowers by Michele, Santa Monica

Many industries follow a standard markup, so you need to find out what that figure is for yours. Quite often, retailers double the wholesale price they paid for an item. So if you are wholesaling your wares, keep that end figure in mind and make sure it is neither too low nor too high. Standard markup can fluctuate, as Linda Wade, owner of the furniture store Putti in Toronto, has found. "Retail margins have fallen since the eighties," she says. "The standard markup used to be about 2.5, now it's about double."

In general, it's a good idea to find an average target markup for your store or operation. Then you may want to vary it, based on factors like whether the item is moving fast or slow, and making sure that you vary it on both sides of the average to balance out in the middle. On slow-moving items, the markup is usually higher to cover the cost of carrying it for longer. On fast-moving items, the markup might be lower to keep prices competitive. You can make up for lower markups by buying certain items more cheaply, and selling them for a higher markup, though still at a competitive rate. "We do our own importing in order to get a better price, and we pass that savings along," says Leeda Marting of Charleston Gardens. "It also allows us to get a better margin. And when a manufacturer gives us a discount, we pass that along."

One final tip on pricing and markup comes from Ann Fox, of Room Service, a home furnishings store in Dallas. "Consider making your initial markup higher so you can discount it or sell it at a sale price later, if necessary, and still make a profit."

VARYING PRICE POINTS AND MARGINS

Although you want your store or retail operation to be consistent and coherent about its target market, for some businesses it's a good idea to carry items in a variety of price ranges. This broadens your market. The perception of Pamela Scurry's Madison Avenue store, The Wicker Garden, is that it caters to upscale customers, but all are welcome and there is a range of prices, from $1,200 silk dresses for babies, to a $35 seersucker toddler outfit. Keep in mind, though, that higher-priced and luxury items require a more skilled sales staff that can assist customers who expect a higher level of service in a more informed way.

On the other hand, you may decide to set your prices all at the same price point level. FACE Stockholm aimed for a medium price point, since their mission in part was to give customers a real alternative to very pricey department-store makeup. With their wide range of color selections and free-spirited approach to beauty, the idea of the company is to make makeup fun for everybody.

If you are a service provider, you may reach the point where it makes business sense to set a minimum on the size of the jobs you'll do. The economies of scale, a term that means that costs (per unit) decline as volume increases, are such that smaller jobs are no longer worth the company's time.

WHEN TO DISCOUNT

Discounting can be part of your pricing strategy. You might consider giving discounts to customers who, in exchange, provide something your business needs. This usually means cash flow. For instance, you might consider offering discounts to customers who pay promptly or up front. Some businesses also offer quantity discounts, especially when the cost-per-unit is reduced by a bulk order. (Economies of scale, again.) This is often the case for caterers and bakers. Before you offer such a discount, it behooves you to figure out the exact quantity at which your costs are reduced and by how much. Businesses that tend to be seasonal, such as inns, usually offer seasonal discounts on the off-season to encourage business during the slow times.

Another reason to discount strategically is your customer will help promote your product. If you are a wholesaler or manufacturer, you might discount an item that your customer, perhaps a store or catalogue, plans to feature prominently in its advertising or is otherwise in a position to promote. For example, FACE Stockholm sells makeup to makeup artists at a discount, since makeup artists obviously can influence consumers of beauty products. Another example: Charleston Gardens asked for and received a discount from the manufacturer of the garden bench it featured on the cover of a recent catalogue. Those savings were passed on to customers.

Sometimes deep discounting is just a way to cut your losses. There's no point in keeping products that are deteriorating or have gone out of style. "When I make a buying mistake," says June Matheson, co-owner of Liberty, a furniture emporium in Vancouver, "I put the mistake out on the floor, in a particular space, with the rest of the mistakes, and mark them down to my costs."

Keeping Records

Entrepreneurs are creative. They want to create and go on to the next creation. We're not maintenance people. When you don't maintain your records, you feel so burdened that you can't create. It's very easy to get in over your head.

—Martina Arfwidson, FACE Stockholm

In many areas of business, there is healthy room for disagreement among successful entrepreneurs. But the importance of good recordkeeping and bookkeeping is one area where there is absolutely no controversy. Those who do it swear by it, and those who don't are full of regret.

There are lots of good reasons for maintaining books and keeping them up to date: to make sure you have priced your products well; to know if you are really making money (just having a lot of customers, being really busy, and making a lot of sales is not necessarily a guarantee of that); to know where your cash is going and how much you have on any given day; to show your bankers, who will definitely want to know where their money is going; and last, but certainly not least, for taxes. Keeping detailed records of expenses, like mileage logged on your car and other travel expenses, will help you get accurate deductions and possibly save you money at tax time. Keeping good books and records helps you avoid unpleasant surprises and even anticipate problems, so that you can take steps to forestall them before things get desperate.

For starters, even if your business is tiny and you are a solo entrepreneur, set up a separate bank account for it, a business account in your own name, if necessary, as long as it is separate from your personal account. Your business checkbook, which should only include records of business expenses, will most likely be your primary source of accounting information. Don't spend personal money on buying things for the business, and vice versa. In addition to keeping the checkbook current (and knowing your balance by heart), it is also a good idea to keep a daily log of all of your business transactions. In business, you have either money in or money out (income or expenses), and both streams need to be recorded, with supporting documents, in a daily log.

To document your income, keep and file invoices, deposit slips, cash-register tapes, credit-card charges, a receipt book.

To document your expenses, keep and file vendor invoices, cancelled checks, cash-register receipts, credit-card charges.

FACE Stockholm's Martina Arfwidson says she even had fun developing a filing system. Here's the system she developed: Each store (three in the United States) keeps a file folder (you could also use an envelope) for each day into which all transaction records, receipts, and credit-card slips go. When the week is up, those folders or envelopes go into a bigger folder. When the month is up, all the folders are placed in chronological order in a white filing carton, and stored with other such cartons.

She has found that among the system's benefits, it helps in dealing with a plaguing business problem—credit-card charge-backs. This is when someone receives a credit-card bill and claims she was charged for something she did not buy. Then the credit-card company calls the business in question to investigate. You not only need proof of what the charges were, you need to be able to put your hands on that day's paperwork to find that proof quickly. "I lost so much money on those at first," says Arfwidson.

For many kinds of businesses, a computer is indispensable for such recordkeeping, but Arfwidson is not convinced that smaller retail establishments need them. "The computer can eat up a lot of time," she says. "We've practically had to have a full-time computer person just to deal with all of the problems." It may be that a daily log kept on paper of all dispersals, income, returns, and comments, as well as a record of who entered the data if you have several people working for you, will serve your business just as well.

Depending on the nature of your business, you may want to establish other systems, computerized or not, for keeping track of what's going on on a daily basis. Certainly, retail and restaurant establishments need to exercise tight inventory control and recordkeeping. Mail-order businesses should record exactly when and how many catalogues went out. Businesses must have a sense of when they can expect fluctuations in sales volume, and the best way of predicting those fluctuations is to record what has happened in previous years or months. Businesses with more than one location need to be able to compare volume at each. Businesses that combine different ways of selling—mail order, phone, web, and storefront—need to compare the different methods. Careful analysis of all this information helps with planning, hiring, marketing, and merchandising.

Collections

Collecting money is one of the biggest hassles in business, but it is vital. If you are not collecting the money that is owed your business, you are jeopardizing both your cash flow and your profits.

The first way to avoid having problems collecting money is to be careful about who you extend credit to. Ask for credit references and check them. Ask customers why they left their previous supplier. Make sure the customer is worth the risk, and follow your instincts about people. Second, set your collection policies or your customers will set them for you—and they won't be in your favor. If you are lax about sending invoices and bills, clients will take all the time in the world to pay you. Don't hesitate to request retainers, deposits, or COD, particularly if someone has been a problem payer in the past.

Making timely collections is another argument in favor of scrupulous recordkeeping. Make sure you have a fail-safe system for filing contracts and purchase orders and a method of following up on uncollected funds. Keep a record of all contacts with the customer you are trying to persuade to pay you until the account is settled and closed. When you send a collection letter, clearly state the amount owed, when it must be paid, and what your next step will be if the account remains delinquent. Should you need to take the extreme step of hiring a collection agency, (which will charge 25 to 50 percent of the amount collected) or going to small-claims court, you'll need all the documentation you've carefully filed along the way.

Setting Up Your Accounting System

To begin with, you will need to set up a chart of accounts. This serves as the basic filing system for all your business's accounting information—a general ledger for your business—and it will also contain the information from which you generate the two most important financial forms: the balance sheet and the income, or profit and loss, statement (more on those below).

Your chart of accounts uses a numbering system to organize all of the accounts or categories that appear on your financial statements. Each account would get its own number, as illustrated below.

BALANCE SHEET ACCOUNTS

1000 Asset Accounts
These are broken down into two kinds:

1000–1499
Current assets—Including cash, receivables, inventory

1500–1999
Fixed assets—Equipment, building, furniture fixtures

2000 Liability Accounts
These are broken down into two kinds:

2000–2499
Current liabilities—Money you owe within a year

2500–2999
Long-term liabilities—Money you owe for more than a year

INCOME STATEMENT ACCOUNTS

3000 Income Accounts
Sales

4000 Direct Expenses
Expenses related to production volume, labor, and materials

5000–6000 Indirect Expenses
Expenses that you have regardless of production

7000–8000 Nonoperating Accounts
These are separate from normal operating expenses and income.
Examples include interest income, income tax.

All of your business activities should fit into these broad categories. You can keep creating numbered files that fall in each category as you invest in new equipment, hire new help, and make new sales. The figures in the chart of accounts are ever changing, and you need up-to-date records and knowledge of them to create accurate financial statements and understand exactly where your business stands. Even fixed assets change in value because of depreciation. (Your accountant can help you establish depreciation schedules for your equipment, vehicles, etc.)

Every transaction should be recorded in the chart of accounts using the double-entry accounting system, which means recording every transaction in two ways: as a debit in one account and a credit in another. For example, if you buy $1,000 worth of inventory, you would debit your cash account by $1,000 and credit your inventory account by $1,000.

By all means, hire a good accountant to set up your accounting system and a scrupulous bookkeeper to maintain it, and make sure that they know exactly how double-entry accounting works, since this is the way businesses keep their balance sheets in order and guard against errors.

The Basics of Financial Statements

In your business plan, you probably created some income projections and budgets based on conjecture. But once your business is up and running, assessing your profit or loss, the net worth of your business, and where the cash actually goes during defined periods of time (weekly, monthly, annually) is no longer a matter of guesswork. It's a matter of diligence and keeping track of the money and making sure everything is recorded with the utmost accuracy.

At first, the keeping of financial records and learning how to read and understand them may seem an arduous, though necessary, chore. Eventually, financial statements will become so familiar to you that you can glance at them and pick out the salient fact or the incipient problem that needs addressing, or zero in on an accounting error. Some entrepreneurs even discover that they enjoy this aspect of their business.

There are three fundamental kinds of financial statements that give you an accurate picture of the overall financial health of your business. They provide you with a wealth of information, alert you to problems in pricing, and allow you to track your progress from month to month and year to year, and give you the vital tools to plan your business for the future.

1. **Balance sheet**—This is a snapshot of where your business stands, and what it is worth (net worth equals what you own minus what you owe). The balance sheet has two columns, one for assets (resources you own) and one for liabilities (debts, expenses you owe). The way you figure out net worth, which is also known as equity, is by subtracting the liabilities from the assets. Generally, balance sheets are completed once a year, unless there is some major change, acquisition or loss, or debt taken on that would necessitate more frequent revision.

The balance sheet provides all sorts of useful information and ratio. One ratio that can be pulled out of the balance sheet is the current ratio. Your current ratio is current assets divided by current liabilities, and it tells you whether your business will be able to pay its bills. Most businesses should aim for a ratio of 2:1 or better. Any less than that, and you may be cutting it too close. It is also possible to have too high a ratio, which would indicate that the business has too much cash sitting around that is not well invested. (See Appendix 4 on page 210 for a sample balance sheet.)

2. **Profit and loss statement** (also P&L or income statement)—This is a monthly statement of sales and expenses, the difference between which will show how much money or profit you made in a given period. You can use P&L statements to track business in a given month, compare it to the same month last year, or place it in the context of how much business you have done so far that year. Total the monthly P&Ls for a year and you get your annual profit (or loss). This is all, obviously, extremely useful information. In a way, the P&L and the balance sheet are two ways of looking at the same information, which is how your business is actually doing as opposed to how busy you are, how hard you are working, how good everything looks, etc. The P&L documents the movement of money into and out of your business, which determines its net worth. (See Appendix 5 on page 211 for a sample P&L statement.)

BALANCE SHEET TEMPLATE

Name of Business:

Date:

Assets:

Current Assets:

- Cash (in business checking, money market, and short-term saving accounts).
- Accounts receivable—money due from customers. As soon as the customer pays, it becomes cash. It is also standard to deduct a certain amount from this figure for doubtful accounts.
- Merchandise/inventory—Goods purchased to be sold at a profit, at which point they become a receivable.
- Prepaid expenses—such as an insurance premium paid in advance.
- Notes receivable—Promissory notes on any loans your company might have made.

Plus Fixed Assets:

- Land
- Building—less accumulated depreciation
- Machinery or equipment—less depreciation
- Fixtures—less depreciation
- Furniture—less depreciation
- Vehicles—less depreciation

Total Assets:

Liabilities:

Current Liabilities: (Current is generally defined as anything that is due within a year.)

- Accounts payable—Money you owe to vendors, contractors, etc.
- Sales tax payable
- Payroll taxes payable
- Accrued wages payable
- Short-term notes payable
- Short-term bank loans payable

Long-term Liabilities:

Long-term Notes Payable:

Mortgage Payable:

Total Liabilities:

Assets – Liabilities = Net Worth

3. Cash-flow statement—Your picture of your business is not complete without a cash-flow statement. This statement chronicles the actual inflow and outflow of cash during a designated period of time, as distinct from when a sale is made or an order taken. It documents your sources and uses of cash. Since cash is the only asset that is liquid and is what you need on hand to pay salaries and bills, a negative cash flow in a business is a full-blown crisis. Profits are nice, but if they are just on paper, they won't pay the bills. Neither will assets like property or inventory, which take time to be liquidated. It is possible to be doing brisk business and still find yourself in a cash crunch. The problem may be one of timing, the bills coming due before customers pay for items they have ordered, for instance. The only way to pinpoint the problem is by keeping regular cash-flow statements (monthly, at least; weekly, even better), which will help you avert and antic-ipate problems. Knowing when bills come due and where the cash to pay them will come from is critical. To do so, you need to record your cash out-flows: checks you write for salaries, supplies, creditors; and your cash inflows: money you get from customers, lenders, and investors.

Apart from keeping cash-flow statements for your own peace of mind, your bank will require them when you try to take out a new loan. The bank wants to know what you do with your cash or what you did with the money they last loaned you. Often, the bank will want to see the cash-flow state-ment divided into three parts:

Operating cash flow—Also known as working capital, this is the money generated from sales and spent on normal operations. This is the most important figure, the lifeblood of the company.

Investing cash flow—The cash generated or spent that is outside of normal operations, investments in equipment or plant, non-recurring gains or losses

Financing cash flow—Cash received or payments made to lenders, investors, shareholders.

Name of Business:
Period/Month:

Beginning cash balance _____

Cash Inflows:

Accounts receivable collections _____
Sales and receipts _____
Collections on loans _____
Other _____

Total cash inflows _____

Cash Outflows (Expenses):

Advertising and promotion
Bank service charges
Credit-card fees
Delivery
Employee benefits
Insurance
Interest
Inventory purchases
Office
Payroll
Payroll taxes
Professional fees
Rent
Supplies
Taxes and licenses
Telephone
Utilities
Other

Total cash outflow_____

Other Cash Inflows or Outflows (Investing and Financing Streams):

Purchase or sale of equipment
Proceeds from or payment of loans
Sale or repurchase of stock
Dividends paid

Ending Cash Balance_____

Budgeting

One of the reasons for keeping good financial records is so that you can budget accurately and effectively. A budget is a numerical version of your business plan, and budgeting, like planning, is something that is ongoing in business. It is also something that you get better at, providing you keep good records and learn from your mistakes. Use your P&L statements to draw up a budget for the next year. Then break down the budget into quarters or better yet, months. Monthly P&L statements provide you with a detailed picture of when business is good and when it is slow. Naturally, your budget and plans for the future will need to take these factors into control. Ultimately, a budget is a tool for you to control your business. You need to budget any time you are thinking of making a change, buying a major piece of equipment, hiring more staff, renting a bigger space, increasing your inventory. A budget is a financial picture of your future, a detailed and realistic plan of your future receipts and expenditures. The budget tells you if you can afford to do what you want to do and if your goals are realistic.

Taxes

By all means, hire yourself a good accountant to do your taxes, but you also need to have a firm handle on the kinds of records you'll need to keep to give to your accountant.

For the self-employed, among the most important records are those that document business expenses, since these will lower the tax burden.

In general, an expense can be deducted if you needed it to operate your business. If you would have incurred the expense even without your business, it's probably not deductible. Another standard for deductibility is whether the expense was ordinary. In other words, would anyone in a similar business incur this expense?

The expense part of your annual P&L statement is a good place to start to get a handle on your business expenses. To the right is a list of possible expenses to guide you in preparing your tax return.

- Advertising costs
- Accounting and bookkeeping fees
- Bank service charges
- Car and truck expenses
- Conferences
- Contract labor
- Credit-card fees
- Depreciation
- Dues
- Education related to your business
- Employee benefits
- Entertainment and business meals (50 percent deductible)
- Equipment
- Freight
- Furniture for office
- Gifts to business associates (up to $25 per person per year)
- Home-office expenses (ask your accountant if you qualify)
- Interest on loans or credit cards
- Legal and professional fees
- Licenses and fees
- Magazine and books related to your business
- Maintenance and repairs on office or retail space
- Office supplies
- Online fees (based on percentage of online time used for business)
- Payroll taxes
- Postage
- Printing and copying
- Rent (of equipment and space)
- Small furnishings and tools
- Telephone (if using a home phone, keep a record of which calls are for work)
- Travel
- Uniforms or special work clothing
- Utilities
- Wages

Once you have a handle on your accounting and a system for keeping track and keeping current, you are free to pursue more creative aspects of running your business. And you don't have to go it alone. The next chapter guides you through the process of choosing and working with the professionals who can keep you straight with the IRS, the law, and help grow your business.

People You Need

If you are not in some type of
team environment, it's hard to
keep moving as much as you
need to in business.

—Sylvia Varney, Fredericksburg Herb Farm

Some small-business people jokingly refer to a disease called "entrepreneuritis." It's an all-too common condition that makes its sufferers reluctant to ask for help or to allow other people to help them, and to think that they alone can and must do everything. The single most repeated piece of advice uttered by successful entrepreneurs is "Don't be afraid to ask for help."

Nobody succeeds in business alone. And no one is in possession of every skill a successful business requires. Even the most independent-minded do-it-yourselfer entrepreneur needs to call in the experts sometimes. Useful help can come in many forms, whether it's friends or family members with business experience who are willing to pitch in to do some grunt work, other entrepreneurs who tell you how they solved a particular problem, mentors offering up the wisdom of experience, or the carefully chosen freelance consultants or professionals you hire.

When you first start up, at the very least you will need the services of two professionals: a lawyer and an accountant.

When Do You Need a Lawyer?

Sole proprietorships are easy enough to form without benefit of legal counsel, but consult a lawyer if you are planning to structure your business as a partnership, limited liability company, or any of the various forms of corporations discussed in Chapter Two. Although partnerships don't necessarily require lawyers, you can save yourself a lot of headaches and possible lawsuits down the road by hiring one to draw up your partnership agreement.

You also need a lawyer to buy or sell real estate, to advise you on any zoning regulations that pertain to you, to help create job applications, to advise you of what regulations for employers you must adhere to, to write employee handbooks, to look over if not create contracts, and to advise you on what kinds of insurance you need to carry to minimize your vulnerability to a lawsuit. Obviously, you'll also need a lawyer if you are sued or are suing someone.

WHAT TO LOOK FOR IN A LAWYER

- Someone you like—intuition and compatibility definitely count.
- Someone who has expertise in corporate and business law, taxes and estate planning. Your lawyer should be something of a generalist but well enough connected to be able to refer you to someone else when necessary.

- Someone who is familiar with your industry, or at least willing to learn more about it. On the other hand, small-business attorney and adviser Cliff Ennico warns, steer clear of the very same lawyer your competitors use. "While the legal code of ethics requires confidentiality," says Ennico, "you don't want to risk an accidental leak of sensitive information."

- Someone who understands your need to keep legal expenses down. This means they should be willing to discuss fees up front and also teach you, or your staff, to handle some of your routine legal matters in-house. Also, ask if they would be willing to assign some of the more routine tasks to a junior associate with a lower hourly fee.

- Convenience and accessibility. You don't want to have to travel half a day to meet with your lawyer. Also, your lawyer should return your calls within a day.

When you are interviewing lawyers, ask lots of questions. If he or she is part of a large firm, ask if that person will be doing most of your work or handing it off to someone else. Make sure you are interviewing the person you'll be dealing with most often.

HOW TO FIND A LAWYER

Ask other small-business owners who they use for their legal needs. Word of mouth from reliable and trusted sources is still the best way to find someone suitable for your type and size business. Your banker or accountant may be able to recommend a lawyer. You might also consult the *Martindale-Hubbell Law Directory*, which contains short bios on each of the entries. Your local bar association will provide you with listings, but not with recommendations.

When Do You Need an Accountant?

A good accountant is essential. You need one who understands you and your business. My accountant was very accessible. He had an office above my first location. You need someone who is at your disposal.

—Paulette Knight, The Ribbonerie, San Francisco

A good accountant should know the ins and outs of tax law as well as the ins and outs of your business. Certainly, you need an accountant when it comes time to file taxes. But your accountant should also advise you on tax planning, which is much more proactive than just filing the proper forms with the IRS. For instance, there are ways you can set up your business that will yield tax savings. Decisions such as how to structure your business; whether to use contract or employee labor; how to structure employee benefits; whether you should hire family members; how to set up your 401K, retirement and health insurance plans; all have tax implications. You should also consult your accountant whenever you are making a major move or purchase, deciding between leasing or buying a piece of equipment, making a deal, selling or relocating your business.

How often you meet with your accountant depends on how complex your finances are. At a very minimum, if yours is a very small business, you should meet with your accountant in October or November to make sure you take advantage of any tax breaks before the end of the year. Meet again toward the beginning of the new year to plan tax-saving strategies for that year. For larger businesses with more complicated finances, meeting every two months, or even monthly, is advisable.

WHAT TO LOOK FOR IN AN ACCOUNTANT

Your accountant should be someone who has expertise in small business—if possible, in your industry—and in start-ups. He or she should also be someone you like and trust. It is advisable to have one accountant for both your personal finances and your business, since this person will be able to see your total financial picture and advise you accordingly. In general, you want an accountant who is proactive, genuinely interested in your financial well-being, and willing to help you take charge of your financial future.

Credentials are good, but don't let them outweigh your gut feelings and instincts. You need to trust and like this person who will know the intimate financial secrets of your business.

HOW TO FIND AN ACCOUNTANT

The same way you find plumbers, lawyers, and good restaurants. Through reliable word of mouth and references from other small-business people.

Professional and trade organizations may also have listings of accountants used by people in your industry. Clothing designer Isabel Garreton recalls her experience:

> References helped me find lawyers and accountants. I stayed away from family for these specific services. I wanted them to relate to my business, not to my family or me. I still chose people I like as people. After fifteen years working together, we still have a friendly relationship.

WHEN YOU NEED MORE THAN AN ACCOUNTANT

If your business grows and takes on many employees and its finances grow too complex for part-time bookkeeping and accounting, you may reach the point where you are consulting your accountant so much you may as well bring him or her on board. Some entrepreneurs do just that. For the combined tasks of preparing financial statements, managing the business's accounts, keeping you straight with the IRS, managing payroll, as well financial planning and analysis, you would probably require someone with an accounting background at minimum. Different businesses call the person who performs or oversees these functions different titles: controller, business manager, general manager, and, in a public company, chief financial officer (CFO).

Consult the Experts, but Rely on Yourself

Finally, no matter how much you trust and rely on the professionals you hire to provide the services needed for your business, remember that no one knows your business as well as you do, or has as much at stake. If someone gives you advice that goes against what you really think will work for your business, follow your gut; make the call that seems right to you. Those who follow advice that goes against their better judgment often rue the day.

Other Professionals and Advisers You'll Need

INSURANCE BROKER

At minimum, you will need property and liability insurance. If you have employees, you'll also need worker's compensation insurance. And if your business owns any vehicles, you'll need to insure them. For all of this, you'll also need a reliable independent insurance broker who can knowledgeably discuss your requirements and help find you the best deals. Joining a trade or professional association may also give you access to some better insurance deals.

Property insurance covers your losses in the event of damage to the building your business is in, or the contents. Just ask Joyce Eddy, the founder of Habersham Plantation, the furniture wholesaler in North Carolina. Her early chances of success were nearly ruined when a fire destroyed her uninsured shop. Liability covers you in the event that someone is injured on your business's premises or by one of your products. Worker's compensation covers employees in the event that they suffer a work-related injury.

PRESS AGENT/PUBLICIST

While a press agent or publicist is not an absolute necessity, publicity is an important part of growing your business, and someone should tend to it, if you do not. A professional publicist or press agent may be able to spread the word about your business and take control of your media image a lot more quickly and effectively than you could, unless you know what you are doing and make it a very high priority. Also, having a good and reputable publicist or public relations firm on board, together with a well-thought-out media strategy, may help you to raise outside money, if you are going that route.

Most publicists work on a monthly flat-fee basis. Some work as independent publicists; others are affiliated with larger publicity firms, which can charge anywhere from $5,000 to $20,000 per month for full service, so hiring a hot publicity firm is a luxury not every start-up business can afford. You may be able to hire a publicity firm for a little less, but often, you get what you pay for. Try to get a month-to-month contract, or the shortest-term-contract possible, so you can cancel if you are not satisfied.

Depending on your budget, one option is hiring a publicist for a limited period of time to accomplish a specific goal. Camilla Bergeron did this when she was launching her antique-jewelry business in the highly competitive climate of Manhattan. She firmly believes that getting the right kind of publicist and publicity can make or break her kind of business. For her, that meant finding someone with expertise and contacts in the fashion-magazine world.

When she was further along in her business, Karen Krasne, of Extraordinary Desserts in San Diego, hired a press agent for one year with the specific goal of getting her business more national exposure. The strategy was successful. Extraordinary Desserts received write-ups in *Bon Appétit* and *Victoria* magazines, and, says Krasne, "It changed my business overnight. I had a 30 percent growth rate."

QUESTIONS TO ASK WHEN SHOPPING FOR A PUBLICIST

(Courtesy of Lisa Linden, CEO of Linden, Alschuler & Kaplan, a New York City-based full-service public relations agency)

1. Who else do they represent? They should be people in your industry, but not direct competitors, which might create a conflict of interests.

2. Are they too busy to service your account? While they should have an impressive client list, they should not be stretched so thin that you can't get your due. Make sure that you know who will be doing the work on your account, and that it is someone relatively senior, not the most recent hire out of college.

3. Do they show enthusiasm for and an understanding of your business? If they yawn or seem bored when you meet them, forget it. Do they listen to you? Do they understand your goals, your customer base, and your audience?

4. Do they have a proven track record with businesses like yours? They should be able to show you clips, TV bits, and placements they have made with online publications. Do they have experience with start-up companies?

5. Do they have good relationships and contacts with the media? Which reporters and editors do they know? Ask for specific names.

6.   Are they media savvy? Do they have good story and news sense? Do they keep up with the news and with trends in your industry. If not, are they willing to? Are they creative in finding angles for how a story could be told?

7.   Do they ask questions and generally exhibit curiosity about your company? They should be exploring different ways to tell your story. They should ask questions about the principals and the history of the company. Do they show creativity and resourcefulness about how they would approach getting you publicity? They should have a variety of techniques—just sending out a lot of press releases is not always the best strategy. Sometimes calling one specific reporter with an exclusive story is much more effective.

OTHER TIPS ON HIRING PUBLICISTS

- Your publicist should be experienced in event planning as well as a first-rate writer. She should also have some abilities in crisis management.

- If you are trying to get publicity for a specific event, hire the publicist at least three to five months beforehand.

- Be prepared to sell yourself to the publicist. It will be hard for her to be as enthusiastic about your business without being sold on it.

- Be prepared to check over any material that publicists send out. You might catch glaring and embarrassing mistakes.

OTHER ENTREPRENEURS

Don't overlook your fellow entrepreneurs as a valuable resource. Even on an informal basis, their accounts of their business experiences will be full of cautionary tales, war stories, and hard-earned wisdom; and unlike lawyers, accountants, and consultants, their advice is free. Other entrepreneurs will also swap tips about new technologies and money-saving ideas that might be germane to your business.

No one understands the demands and challenges of starting your own business as well as someone who has been there. Join trade associations and organizations of women entrepreneurs if you have trouble finding such people. (Consult the Resources section at the end of this book for listings of such organizations.) When you meet other entrepreneurs, don't be afraid to ask questions about some of the troubling aspects of your business. At the very least, you'll realize that you are not alone. At best, someone might just be in possession of the perfect solution to your problem.

MENTORS

Some people are lucky enough to find mentors along the way, perhaps a teacher or a boss they have admired who encouraged them and saw their potential. Wakefield, Rhode Island–based designer Monica Schaeffer first sold her imaginative freeform wreaths through other women's stores. One of these women encouraged Schaeffer to strike out on her own and open her own store. It was an extra dose of confidence that Schaeffer needed when she finally opened her whimsical shop, Wild Child.

Diane Forley, the young restaurateur who owns Verbena in Manhattan, says her father is her biggest supporter and best mentor. His business was jewelry, not fine food, but, "He was the one who made me think it was possible to own my own business," says Forley.

Just because you haven't fallen into a mentoring relationship doesn't mean you should not make an effort to find one. Seasoned entrepreneurs like Mary Ella Gabler, owner of Peacock Alley, supplier of luxury linens, says that the current climate of business is so complicated that it's foolhardy to try to weather it alone. "I learned everything from scratch," she says. "I really don't recommend that."

Make it a point to find someone you admire, who also admires you. Ideally, a mentor should be someone who is much farther along on the path you are embarking on, someone who has nothing to fear from you competitively. Once you zero in on someone like that, consider calling or dropping a note asking to get together and chat, explaining that you are impressed by what she is doing. Diane Forley somewhat brazenly called the owners of restaurants she admired when she was in the planning stages of her own restaurant. She asked to see their business plans and for whatever advice they could offer. Many of them, flattered, obliged.

Joining a trade association is another way to find a mentor, says Ellen

Rohr, author of two books on small-business money matters, who also teaches seminars to small-business people. "The primary reason for joining is so you can find successful people with whom you don't compete. Get together as mastermind partners. Compare financial data and marketing strategies. Commit to help each other. Find the most successful person in your industry and ask for help. Most successful people are very generous with their information because no one gets to the top without help. They understand it's time for them to help someone else."

A mentor-protege relationship does not have to be permanent. You might want to seek out a mentor or some other kind of advice when you are trying to make a transition in your business, whether starting up, changing direction, or expanding.

MASTERMIND GROUP

The term "mastermind group" comes from Napoleon Hill's *Think and Grow Rich*, the classic self-help reference book some entrepreneurs still swear by, including Charleston-based dress and soft-accessory designer Cookie Washington. She says her mastermind group consists of good friends, "women who sympathize with me, and who are honest with me, and who serve as a kind of informal think tank. They are people to bat around ideas with."

Washington credits her mastermind group with talking her out of an idea that she now sees was awful. "I was going to specialize just in wedding dresses for plus-sized women," she says. She has subsequently realized that focus was too narrow. Washington also consulted her mastermind group when she first opened her studio in her home. She asked them: "Is this studio warm and inviting? Do I look professional?"

ADVISORY PANEL

You could take a step farther and consider putting together a more formal advisory board, made up of thinkers and leaders, successful people in business, or just people whose ideas you respect, who have also expressed interest in and admiration for you and your business. To make the arrangement more formal, you can make them members of your board, hold quarterly or semi-annual meetings, and even offer them a stipend for attending what are essentially brainstorming sessions for your business.

When she wanted to explore new directions to take her business, including books, TV, and branding, Manhattan-based floral and garden designer Rebecca Cole assembled an advisory board made up of what he calls an "amazing group of women," including an entertainment lawyer, a literary agent, and an Internet entrepreneur. Several had been former clients of Cole's. "I got them together because I had been advised by all of them over the years. They are all really busy people, so I sent a car for one of them and served them wine. The first time we did it, they all said, 'This was amazing, let's do it again.'"

TIPS ON GETTING THE MOST OUT OF MENTORS AND ADVISERS

- Know what you want. Have a specific agenda when you get together.
- Develop a specific plan of action with your mentor/advisers.
- Decide together on the level of structure you want in the relationship, and on the guidelines, i.e., impromptu telephone calls at home, or formal regular meetings.

WHO ELSE DO YOU NEED?

Take the advice of Debbie DuBay, of Limoges Antiques in Andover, Massachusetts: "Don't forget the property manager, who is better than your husband for fixing your sign, etc. And get to know the local police who are a must for keeping an eye on you and your small business."

PEOPLE YOU DON'T NEED

It should go without saying, but too often, for women, it does not. As small-business guru Jane Applegate of SBTV.com says, "Don't work with people who make you sick." You will likely encounter people who are negative about what you are doing, or who try to sabotage your efforts in all sorts of devious ways. (With any luck, they won't be related to you.) If they work for you, fire them. If you work for them, make this the last job you do for them.

If you work with them, sever the relationship.

"Surround yourself with positive people," advises designer and events planner Pat Kerr. "Keep negative thoughts out. Don't let other people sabotage you."

Supportive Friends and Family

Certainly, starting and running a business, like any other endeavor, is made easier with the support of a loving family. This does not mean that you cannot succeed in business without one—many women entrepreneurs started their businesses in the wake of divorces, out of financial necessity. Single woman entrepreneurs and single mother entrepreneurs are not at all uncommon. Monica Schaffer was newly divorced, with three young children to support when she started her floral design business, Wild Child, in Wakefield, Rhode Island. Helen Cox had been buying and selling silver on a small scale for a few years, but when she got divorced, she became serious about business, and opened As You Like It Silver Shop in New Orleans. A single mother, with modest farm-country roots, Joyce Eddy built her wholesale furniture empire, Habersham Plantation, in North Carolina through sheer hard work and self-reliance. Eventually, her eldest son joined her in running the business.

Whatever the experts may say, it is not unusual for family members to step in and help out with the work needed in a small business. "Working with family is not recommended, especially in this culture," says clothing designer Isabel Garreton. "But I find it difficult to grow a small business without family involvement. Sacrifice is part of building a business and often family steps in. This is to be appreciated, not taken advantage of."

Many women entrepreneurs work with dear old mom, counting her as their right-hand employee. "I had my own mother ironing for me," says Marsha Manchester, of Milady's Linens in New Hampshire. "She didn't do the job as well as I did so I had to 'let her go'! I hired her to be the cashier and bagger, a job she loved."

In Martina Arfwidson's case, it was her mom, Gun Nowak, who started the company, FACE Stockholm, the retailer of boldly colored, moderately priced makeup and nail polish. Though Arfwidson had planned a career in musical theater, she ended up going into business with her mom. The two women share a vision for the company—for example, they agreed not to have their stores in malls or department stores—and remain extremely close.

As with any partnership, that between family members or husbands and wives seems to work better when the talents are complementary rather than competitive. "Sallie and I couldn't imagine running this business without one another," says Margaret Jones, who, with her sister Sallie, owns Scriptura, a fine-paper emporium in New Orleans. "She and I each contribute distinctly different talents to this business and somehow come together to make a perfect whole. Since we wear different hats, we rarely fight and are very dependent on one another. Our experience in partnership has been ideal. We know, however, that we are lucky and this is not the case for everyone."

Husband and wife partnerships are often strewn with minefields. Working with a spouse means constant togetherness and increased difficulty in separating your home and work lives. When you work with a spouse, you may end up seeing sides of him that you never knew existed. Likewise, he will see some hidden sides of you. As Princeton, Wisconsin-based home decor designer Tracy Porter says about being in business with her husband, John, "You think you know someone until you see how they are when they conduct business." She also says that she and John have made a firm commitment to one another that the marriage comes first. "I would never pretend to paint a picture that we have it all perfectly figured out; we're still learning every single day."

Sylvia Varney, co-owner with her husband of Fredericksburg Herb Farm, concedes that the business is hard on the marriage. "Integrity and honesty are important, and you have to be willing to compromise. You also have to address the uncomfortable issues."

Though it may seem that much less needs to be said and formalized when you work with family members or a spouse, the very opposite may be the case. Clean-cut delineations of responsibilities beforehand can save a lot of wear and tear on both the relationship and the business. For instance, who will handle emergency child care or other home emergencies? Who will handle business emergencies if you are both on vacation?

HIRING FAMILY AND FRIENDS

When you are starting a small business, it is only natural that you will call on friends and family members to help and contribute. There is nothing inherently wrong with that as long as you do not take advantage of people. Family businesses have thrived since the beginning of time and will likely continue to do so. After all, whom can you trust more than family to keep the books, mind the store, and collect the cash?

Generally, some experts say, hiring people you know or are related to works out best when the friend or family member in question has some skill that is complementary to yours. And before hiring a friend or family member, you should also consider whether you will be able to treat this person as an employee and whether your personal relationship with that person will put a strain on other valued employees. Dinnerware designer Gail Pittman says she is extremely sensitive to these issues when it comes to hiring her own grown children. "I don't agree with bringing your children into the business unless they start from the bottom and work their way up," she says. "It's just not fair to the other people who work for you."

Many entrepreneurs caution against hiring friends, none more strongly than Margaret Jones, of Scriptura paper emporium. "Don't hire friends," she says. "At first it seems nice to have them around, but ultimately, it is very hard to ask them to do things. Work seems to go the best with people who have no direct correlation to your personal life."

So whom should you hire and how can you spot a good prospect? The following chapter discusses the ins and outs of staffing your growing enterprise.

Hiring Staff

*Hire very good people to do
the stuff you cannot do.*

—Claire Murray, designer

As your business grows, at some point, so does your need for staff. You will have to let go of certain tasks and delegate them to other people whom you hire and pay to do the work. It can be difficult to relinquish even the tiniest aspect of a company you have created from scratch and nurtured into existence. You may have become accustomed to doing everything yourself in your own way. Ultimately, by freeing you to do the things that you are really good at—and needed for—delegating responsibilities to other people can be personally liberating as well as a smart and necessary move for your business. At the same time, hiring and managing staff adds a new dimension to your responsibilities as a business owner.

As any businessperson will tell you, having the right staff can make or break a business. Most important, you need to have a solid core of people on whom you and your business can depend. It is also likely that your staff will all too often be in a state of flux, as people's lives change and they move on to other ventures and challenges. Finding and keeping the right people is something you will be doing on an ongoing basis.

Whether you have just a few people working for you or dozens, issues surrounding staffing and the people who work for you will consume a great deal of your time and energy. "You deal with personnel issues all the time, no matter how big you get," says Mary Ella Gabler of Peacock Alley, purveyor of luxury linens. "I have a human resources person working for me and I still deal with it all the time. You have to listen, analyze, and pay close attention to all the sides of the story. You have to be very fair."

The painful truth is that only the truly exceptional hired hand will ever care quite as much, be as committed to, or be as motivated about your business as you. And those employees are almost impossible to find. Nevertheless, through a variety of techniques, good instincts, and a little bit of luck, many business owners manage to put teams in place that work for them and their business.

Learning to Delegate

What are you good at, and what does your business really need you to do? These are some of the questions you should ask yourself when you begin to think about delegating tasks and hiring people to help you. If you have been running your business single-handedly, you have probably had a chance to dabble in nearly every aspect, from design to sales to marketing to ordering supplies. If some of those burdens were put on other shoulders, it might free you up to take your business to the next level.

At the same time, hiring staff is something you should approach cautiously. Taking on employees is a big responsibility. Don't overhire. Don't farm out too much responsibility. And don't do it too early. For instance, just because you have a good bookkeeper and accountant does not absolve you of the need to understand your business's budget, financial needs, and cash-flow status and expectations. You need to know enough to oversee all the areas of your business.

And just because you have some people working for you does not mean that you will never have to pick up the slack. For morale, and sometimes out of sheer necessity, you still have to show a willingness to do even the least glamorous jobs. Kate Flax of Kate's Paperie often finds herself opening cartons of supplies for hours. And no entrepreneur can afford to be above emptying the garbage or preparing a package to be shipped.

On the other hand, once you hire people, make sure that you let them do the jobs they have been hired to do. Give them genuine responsibility; don't micromanage them, or treat them as children.

Determining What You Need

The first step on the road to hiring staff is defining exactly what you need, and what you can afford. You may just need to hire a freelancer on a temporary basis to help you through a busy time or your busy season. Perhaps you have a job whose workload could be handled by someone part-time, or flex-time. Or, have you reached the point where your company is growing, is braced to grow more and needs to increase its full-time staff.

Whether you are writing a want ad, or spreading the word that you are looking to hire some other way, you'll need to come up with a job description. A job description should include the title, overall purpose, specific tasks and duties, and the role this job plays in the company. Consult your budget and research the going rate to figure out a ballpark salary, or in the case of a freelance contractor, fee structure.

Real life does not always cooperate, but avoid haste in hiring whenever you can. "Desperation in hiring is worse than being understaffed," says Michele Rosier, owner of Flowers by Michele in Santa Monica. "I'd rather work two times as hard than get stuck with a nightmare employee."

Contract Labor versus Full-Time Employees

Businesses small and large often try to fill staffing needs by using contract labor rather than full-time employees. The reasons are clear: Contract labor is less expensive for the business, since independent contractors (i.e., free-lancers) are not entitled to the benefits staff members receive and they are responsible for paying their own taxes. However, the IRS has become increasingly suspicious of these arrangements, since some companies have abused the system.

Independent contractors work for more than one person, set their own hours, invoice you for the job, and usually provide their own tools.

If you are the sole employer, dictating the person's hours, providing training, and closely supervising their work, chances are that person has crossed over into being an employee. "If it looks, smells, and acts like an employee," says small-business attorney, Cliff Ennico, "then that's probably what it is."

If you decide that you need to take on full-time employees, you need to consult a lawyer to see which federal and state regulations apply to you. The more employees, the more regulations. At minimum, you will be subject to:

The Fair Labor Standards Act, which regulates minimum wage, standard work week and overtime rules.

Social Security—You'll need to get all employees social security numbers and an employer ID number from the IRS.

Medicare/FICA—Health insurance from the federal government, which is paid jointly by the employer and employee.

Federal Unemployment Tax Act, which covers employees who lose their jobs.

Finding People: Word of Mouth and Advertising

When looking for employees, business owners often begin by casting their nets fairly close to home. They find people through word of mouth, referrals from friends, relatives, or acquaintances. Sometimes, shopowners might hire repeat customers who have shown a particular affinity for their business.

To widen the circle, want ads are an effective option. Like any advertisment, these need to be placed in the appropriate publication, probably a local one, and convey the necessary information: job title, brief description of responsibilities, necessary skills, salary range, and contact information. If you have a web site, you should probably post career or job opportunities at your company. But you will probably still have to advertise the job in the local paper (along with web site information).

NONTRADITIONAL WORKERS

Some businesses have begun to tap nontraditional labor pools, such as senior citizens, teenagers, and welfare-to-work clients. These types of hires can work out well for everyone involved, especially when additional support and mentoring are provided for employees who are less familiar with the working world.

Another way to attract good people is by offering flex-time positions, which often appeals to mothers of small children. Mothers, fathers, or other people who have a full plate of personal demands may well have impeccable credentials and skills but want more time with their families. Say, for example, you have decided you need a controller about three days a week instead of a full-time bookkeeper. A good controller would most likely have a CPA and graduate business education and would be able to take your business to the next level in terms of financial statements, planning, and analysis. This may be a job you could offer to the right candidate on a flex-time basis.

Also, businesses in or near college towns frequently hire college students for entry-level jobs. Energetic young people can make good employees, although a relatively high degree of turnover is inevitable with this population.

PEOPLE LIKE YOU

It is natural to be drawn to and hire people who are very much like you. In some cases, this can be a good idea. You may want someone with an upbeat disposition similar to yours and a comparable level of customer-friendliness minding the store when you are not there. The futurist Faith Popcorn advises hiring people who share a sense of your business's mission. This also means that you should communicate the mission to prospective employees.

Manhattan-based floral and garden designer Rebecca Cole offers the seemingly unorthodox advice of hiring people with ambitions to start a business similar to yours, since they make for extremely motivated employees. "It's hard not to be threatened by that," she says. "But something would have to be seriously wrong with your business if they were able to start their own and steal all your customers."

PEOPLE NOT AT ALL LIKE YOU

There are also positions for which you should hire someone whose personality and skills are completely different from yours. The right person for the job might be someone who you would never dream of spending time with outside of work. Michele Rosier, of Michele's Flowers in Santa Monica, says she was initially put off and even intimidated by the woman she eventually hired as her general manager, who came to her through a family friend. She now considers her one of the best hires she ever made, since she and her general manager have complementary skills and personalities.

Some people are organizational people; others are sales oriented. Decide what you are looking for and find out what makes a person tick before you hire her.

—Margaret Jones, Scriptura, fine-paper emporium, New Orleans

Interviewing Techniques

When you are interviewing prospective employees, be prepared, professional, and honest. Being prepared means, first and foremost, knowing what you are looking for, what job needs to be filled. You should have in mind not only the skills you are looking for, but also the kind of background and approach to business. Then you need to develop questions that will tease out this information.

BE PREPARED

Prepare a standard list of questions beforehand to make sure you cover the bases. When you ask questions about previous jobs, try to make them open-ended, so that the answers will reveal as much as possible about the person's responsibilities, behavior, and way of working. Ask what the toughest aspect of the job was, and how she dealt with that. How she organized or juggled different tasks. Try to formulate questions that will make the person think and have to display her problem-solving skills. Ask how she would handle a difficult situation that is bound to arise on the job, for instance, a hard-to-please customer, or thorny delivery problem. Paint a scenario drawn from real experience, and ask her to offer a solution, or a way of tackling it.

If you are interviewing multiple candidates, ask them all a standard list of questions so you can compare their responses. Listen carefully to both their answers and whatever questions the applicants ask. Look for people who show some sense of the big picture of your business and how they would fit in. Make notes right after the interview of salient points of each candidate.

BE PROFESSIONAL

By all means, be friendly and natural and cordial, but stick to job-related questions, not personal ones. Also, don't do all or even most of the talking. Experts recommend that you, the interviewer, do about 20 percent of the talking, letting the candidates talk the other 80 percent of the time. For one thing, you don't want to give them so much detailed information that they can tailor their answers to suit you. For another, you won't learn anything about them if you talk the whole time. When they talk about past jobs, look for patterns in their speech or behavior that provide clues about how they would approach a job working with you. If they don't answer your questions, keep probing until they do.

The fact that you spend most of your time listening does not mean you shouldn't answer their questions, preferably at the end of the interview. In fact, good candidates should have some questions for you, and the nature of their questions should provide you with still more clues about them.

BE HONEST

You might be able to save yourself from hiring someone who is a poor fit, by being frank about what it is really like to work for you and for your company.

I always tell people in interviews exactly what I am like to work for. I try to be very open. I'll say, "I'm good at this, and not good at this. I'm usually running around doing a trillion things, so if you need me, you need to reach out and ask me, because I may not ask you. Are you comfortable communicating like that?"

—Martina Arfwidson, FACE Stockholm

Also, if you say you'll be making a decision within two weeks, and will call them to let them know, be sure that you do.

WHAT TO LOOK FOR

Either in the interview, or when you are checking references, ask questions that will give you a sense of whether an applicant has the following attributes, which will be helpful not only to you but also to co-workers:

1.   The ability to see the big picture, and how their particular job fits into the whole

2.   The ability to follow through

3.   The willingness to help

4.   Overall pleasantness

As you before more proficient in hiring, you will develop a sense of what you are looking for in an employee. An instant turnoff for Martina Arfwidson, for example, is a candidate who has bounced from job to job. "I look for longevity in other jobs," she says. For Arfwidson, loyalty is important.

Cake designer Charmaine Jones hires more cake-decorating help during her busy (wedding) season. "An art background is always good," she says. And she also asks questions about applicants' hobbies to find out if they enjoy activities that require patience and a steady hand, like knitting and crocheting.

Nancy Clark, the proprietress of the Old Chatham Sheepherding Inn, a restaurant, inn, farm, and retail business in Old Chatham, New York, boils her hiring philosophy down to three simple words: "Hire happy people."

WHAT NOT TO ASK

You could, quite innocently, stumble into a legal quagmire by asking the wrong or inappropriate questions during an interview. When in doubt, before asking a question, ask yourself if it is job-related. Here's a partial list of topics to avoid, all of which can be construed as discriminatory, during an interview:

- age (Avoid even the use of the word "overqualified" with older applicants.)
- race
- ethnicity
- religion
- citizenship (You may, however, ascertain whether the person can legally work in this country.)
- ancestry
- birthplace
- height or weight (unless clearly related to the job)
- whether the person owns or rents his or her home
- medical history
- pregnancy
- marital status
- sexual preference
- child-care arrangements
- physical or mental disabilities
- arrest record (You can, however, ask about convictions.)

WHEN IS A TEST APPROPRIATE?

For certain kinds of jobs, testing potential employees may be appropriate. Dinnerware designer Gail Pittman, for example, administers an art test to candidates applying for jobs handpainting the dinnerware. Pittman says the purpose of the test is twofold: to demonstrate artistic ability and to see how well the applicant follows instructions. "We need people who pay careful attention to what we say."

If you are going to test potential employees, be prepared to justify why the test is necessary, and make sure that it is designed to test relevant skills. The best kind of test, like Pittman's, is one that involves a piece of the job itself.

GOOD COP/BAD COP

When you narrow the field to two or three candidates, it is a good idea to have someone else whose opinions and instincts you trust but who might have a different point of view interview them. "I'm softhearted and my general manager is a toughie," says Michele Rosier, of Flowers by Michele in Santa Monica. "I would recommend having more than one other person meet with people you're thinking of hiring."

Hiring Mistakes

Everyone makes hiring mistakes, and everyone seeks methods to avoid them. There is probably no foolproof method, but for some entrepreneurs, learning to trust their instincts can avoid mistakes. Others implement a system of multiple interviews, hiring on trial bases, and testing people. But even with the best-formulated hiring plans, mistakes are bound to happen.

> *"We have learned that it is imperative to check references and listen to our instincts when hiring someone. After interviewing a potential employee, you should take time to digest the information you have learned about that person and listen to the little voice in the back of your mind that usually tells you whether or not the person is a good fit. We made a lot of mistakes hiring people. Some of the people did not like each other, which made the atmosphere in our store very uncomfortable for everyone else.*
>
> —Helen Cox, As You Like It Silver Shop, New Orleans

LETTING PEOPLE GO

> *Letting people go is such a hard thing. When you are a small company, you get personally involved with people who work for you. Even when I have caught people stealing from me, I have a hard time with confrontation. It's horrible. I've finally had to convince myself that it's not for me personally that someone has to be fired. It's for the health of the company. Women entrepreneurs don't draw the line early enough, and we suffer for it. We have to say "no" sooner.*
>
> —Martina Arfwidson, FACE Stockholm

Sometimes you have no choice but to fire an employee. Firing people is not something that anyone relishes, but it is, unfortunately, an inevitable part of running a business with employees. There are essentially three reasons for firing people: poor performance, cutbacks necessitating layoffs, and what is technically called "termination for cause," which generally means a problem with the person's conduct. All three broad categories of firing require documentation leading up to it. In a well-run business, being fired for poor performance should not come as a great surprise to anyone. Prior to the firing, the employee should have received warnings, both verbal and written, and reasonable opportunities to improve their performance, all of which should be documented.

Before firing someone, prepare what you are going to say. If you are really nervous about it, or anticipate some resistance or other complication, consider role-playing with someone beforehand. Be prepared for any questions the person being fired might have. Be firm and courteous, and make it clear that the firing is final. Tell them the truth of why they are being fired, as long as it is nothing personal. Avoid apologizing, and don't engage in an argument. If you anticipate a problem, have a witness with you.

Finally, be sensitive to appearances when firing people. If you fire two older workers in a row, someone might argue you have a pattern of discriminating against older workers. Be careful not to even appear unfair in your firing and hiring, even if your motives are above reproach.

> I think you know within 30 days whether you've hired the wrong person. We give a 90-day trial period, for the sake of both parties.
>
> —Mary Ella Gabler, Peacock Alley

TRIAL PERIODS

One safeguard against hiring mistakes is implementing a trial period. Someone who is wrong for the job may be able to make it through the interview process, but it is unlikely that they will make it through a reasonable trial period. These can be presented as very much in the interests of both parties. Just make sure that the hire understands that until the trial period is complete, there is no guarantee.

Employee Benefits

Competitive salary and benefits are, of course, part of what will attract quality employees. Although everyone would love to offer the most generous benefits possible, many small businesses will find these difficult to afford.

One option is to offer a flexible benefits package, where employees are offered a lump sum for benefits and then a menu of options to choose from for their package. To figure out what kind of benefits your business can and should offer, consult with your accountant.

COMMISSIONS VERSUS SALARY RAISES

Salespeople are often motivated by money, and for many businesses, developing a commission system that rewards initiative and sales is an excellent tool. Before you implement a commission system, consider that it will also impact your customers. Salespeople working on commission can be pushier and more competitive with one another, and can set a very different tone that may be inappropriate to your store. You may want to raise salaries as a way of motivating and keeping good people instead.

> *I hire everyone on a three-month trial basis. They might not be happy, and I might not be. Unhappy people drag everyone else down.*
>
> —Martina Arfwidson, FACE Stockholm

EMPLOYEE MANUALS

About five years into her business, Karen Krasne, owner of Extraordinary Desserts in San Diego, created an employee manual. "I felt we needed more structure and to be more professional," she says. Diane Forley, owner of Verbena restaurant in Manhattan, also discovered that despite her initial inclination to be flexible she soon needed to set down clear employee policies.

Small-business experts say creating an employee manual or handbook is advisable for every business. Many misunderstandings, and even lawsuits, can be avoided by setting down the company's policies on paper and making sure all employees are familiar with them.

Employee manuals are often lengthy documents spelling out the policies and procedures regarding employment at your company. They are often prepared by a lawyer specializing in employee manuals or by a human resources specialist. Some of the items included are:

1. An acknowledgment form, indicating that the person hired has read the manual, agrees to its terms, and also agrees that she is an "employee at will," meaning that she can be fired without cause. (Whether or not you have an employee manual, it's important that all hires sign this kind of acknowledgment. See Appendix 6 on page 212 for a sample form.) If you have a trial-basis policy, you also need to get the hiree to sign something agreeing to that.

2. A welcome statement, a mission statement, and some background on the company.

3. An outline of your company's policies regarding

   - attendance
   - sick leave and time off
   - vacation—how much, how vacation accrues, and when employees must notify you they are taking vacation
   - holidays
   - use of company property, i.e., phones, computers, Internet, etc.
   - dress codes
   - confidentiality about clients or techniques you are using
   - payroll information, including information about pay periods and options like direct deposit
   - work hours—when employees are expected to arrive and leave, how long lunch is, how they report their hours
   - benefits package—how it works, who is entitled to it
   - safety and accident rules—information about worker's compensation
   - substance abuse, sexual harassment, and smoking
   - how and when salaries and performance will be reviewed
   - other items as they apply: employee purchases, idea incentive programs, etc.

Motivating and Managing People

You will have a company of people who are exactly the way you make them. If you are a micromanager, you'll have a company of people who cannot make a move without your telling them exactly what to do. Instead of telling people who answer the phone that they must answer it before the third ring, I started to say, "Your job is to make every client who talks to you think that this is the most helpful company in the world." And then let them figure out how to get there. It's better to say to your employees, "We're on a team together with this as our goal."

—Rebecca Cole, Rebecca Cole Designs, Manhattan

Hiring the right people is only the beginning. Managing, motivating, and keeping the good ones is also a major and ongoing challenge. You will constantly be called upon to hone your management skills as a business owner who leads a staff. As the owner of the business, your motivation to make it succeed and your passion for it are seldom in question. Some staff members may be passionate about their jobs, which is a huge bonus, and you should certainly try to hire people who are passionate about the work they will do for you. But when the passion flags, here are some pointers about maintaining motivation among your staff.

- Be clear with your expectations and in conveying what employees' responsibilities are. This starts with creating good job descriptions, but over time, these descriptions may evolve. Be sure to communicate any changes clearly.

- Let employees share in the decision-making.

- Keep them informed about what's going on in the company, either through staff meetings or an employee newsletter.

- Be as approachable as possible, and try to have an open-door policy. Stay tuned to what's going on with the employees. If there is a dip in morale, address it. Listen to what employees have to say. You might even implement an idea incentive program to reward and encourage employees to come up with ideas that help the business.

- Remember to praise employees and otherwise reward good work.

- Work on your ability to give constructive criticism. Criticism should never be personal or even borderline abusive. If you have any difficulty with holding your temper, do whatever it takes to learn how to manage it. Angry outbursts from the person in charge can poison the atmosphere of any business.

- Don't micromanage. Give your employees the big picture and trust them to know how to get there. If they can't, you may have made a bad hire in the first place. Give well-chosen staff members authority and responsibility. That will make the job more interesting to them and genuinely relieve you of some burdens.

- Let people do what they are good at. Don't try to force them into roles in the company just because you need it filled. Know their limits.

Retail Staffing

When it comes to hiring people to work in my store, first of all, strong intuition is helpful. Trusting a person to run my store is liking trusting them to take care of my child. When I feel I've selected the right applicant, training them in all the areas is essential. Also, the character of the person should fit your type of store. They have to want to work there and enjoy their job. I have hired only by referral or a sign in the window. If they come into the store, they know right away if they want to work there.

—Gail Smith Peterson, Buckingham Mercantile, Cardiff-by-the-Sea, California

One of the key elements of our success in keeping quality people is that we have created a familylike atmosphere. Everyone likes each other. We celebrate birthdays with a cake; sometimes, we all go out to dinner for special occasions. Of course, we have a Christmas party in which the families are included. We treasure our employees and we regard their happiness as essential to a pleasant atmosphere for us as well as our customers. We also are accepting of our employees' mistakes (within limits) as being human.

—Helen Cox, As You Like It Silver Shop, New Orleans

No one has more staffing headaches than retailers. Getting and keeping good people in a field that generally pays modestly, even at the high end, is a challenge that becomes downright acute in a robust economy. Ask a retailer how she handles staffing and you can generally be assured you'll first hear a groan, then her comments accompanied by a note of exasperation. "Getting dedicated people is very difficult," say Linda Wade, owner of Putti, a store of antiques and home furnishings in Toronto.

The more upscale the retail establishment, the more training is generally required, which limits the labor pool even further. Paula Goldstein, of Desana, a small, personalized-fragrance store in Boston, has experienced similar frustrations with keeping people, and acknowledges that there may be no getting around the high turnover rate in retail. Her advice on keeping people: "Treat them as human beings. Be aware of their needs. If they ask for something, don't automatically say no. If someone's not feeling good, send them home. And don't dock their pay."

Pam Scurry, of Wicker Garden in Manhattan, also weighs in on the side of treating her retail staff as humanely as possible. She's closed on Sundays, something of a rarity for stores in Manhattan, and closes on Saturdays in July and August to give employees somewhat longer summer weekends. She also offers a generous employee discount, and everyone gets a bonus if the business grows appreciably.

KEEPING A RETAIL STAFF MOTIVATED

Kate Flax, owner of Kate's Paperie in Manhattan, on motivating her staff:

- By example: "I try to motivate my staff by example. There's nothing I don't do in my shop. I'll work with the receiving manager and open cartons for five or six hours sometimes."

- By incentives: "If we have something we really want to move, we offer commissions."

- By praise: "You can't tell them enough how much you appreciate them."

- By pay: "We pay more than average."

- By training: "I try to make it interesting for them, to make them grow, and learn about paper. We also promote from within."

- By caring: "I often bring in cookies, and we never forget a birthday."

Having a happy, skilled and productive staff will make the task of growing your business not only possible, but pleasurable. Expect to make mistakes, learn from them, and move on. You and your business will both survive and thrive if you do.

The First Year and Beyond:
Growing, Changing, Making Mistakes

The first year in business is like the first year of your first child. The excitement and love keep you going over the hurdles, sometimes easily, sometimes stumbling with the exhaustion of this newly acquired responsibility. When everybody is sleeping you are still awake, in charge of the outcome, but if somebody asks, "Would you rather not have it?" the excitement wins and you reply, "Never."

—Isabel Garreton, clothing designer,
Rancho Palos Verdes, California

When you first start your business, expect all of the highs and lows of a life lived on an emotional roller coaster. It may seem that there is very little middle ground between highs like a successful grand opening, landing a big account, the first favorable write-up, and a brimming cash register, and lows like several slow days in a row, a shipment that is two months late, and the exhaustion of near round-the-clock work. The first year, everything is new. Expect to have your mettle tested and your previous ideas on what running a business would be like to go through an ongoing reality check.

> *When one door closes another door opens; but we often look so long and so regretfully upon the closed door that we do not see the ones which open for us.*
>
> —Alexander Graham Bell

The first year of business is, among other things, an intensive learning process. You might even think of the money you've invested in your business as tuition. You're getting a hands-on education that most business schools cannot teach. If you are making money, or even breaking even, you're getting that education for quite a bargain.

If there is a fundamental flaw in your business idea and plan, like an underlying unprofitability, but your research has failed to expose the flaw, the cold slap of reality will hit in your first year. Less catastrophically, you may have overestimated or otherwise misunderstood the market and need to make adjustments quickly. For whatever reason, perhaps people are not as head-over-heels in love with your product(s) as you are or perhaps you've chosen too narrow a market niche. Making mistakes in the first year is not necessarily lethal, but failing to recognize and learn from them is.

In business, as in comedy, timing is everything. You may discover you have tapped into a rich vein of consumer desire, and quickly become overwhelmed with demand. Marsha Manchester caught the early wave of the antiques craze when she opened her first antique linen and furniture shop in New Hampshire a little more than thirty years ago. "It seemed that I could do nothing wrong," she remembers. "As soon as I stripped and refinished a piece of furniture, it would be sold. I had back orders for linens, lamps, kitchenware, and furniture."

Early success is a lot more fun than early struggles, but success can come with its own peculiar struggles, crises, and crunches. If you aren't prepared for it, you may not be in the position to capitalize on it. Another pitfall, you might get swept in a direction you never wanted to go.

Reacting Versus Being Proactive: A Case Study

TRACY PORTER AND STONEHOUSE FARM GOODS: THE HOME COLLECTION

Tracy Porter had always been creative and loved to design and make beautiful household objects. When a tray she created for a soon-to-be wed friend made a big splash at a bridal shower, Tracy and her new husband, John, made the somewhat impulsive decision to go to the New York Gift Show and try to sell Tracy's trays. The response was so overwhelming that they were in business before they had a business plan, a staff, or anything resembling a manufacturing operation. Before long, they had built a studio, hired fifty people and started manufacturing. They also opened a store, Stonehouse Farm Goods, in Princeton, Wisconsin, to display and sell their wares.

There was just one hitch. Tracy and John had come to realize they did not really want to be in manufacturing. What they really wanted was to design beautiful collections and license them to other manufacturers. In a painful, but, for them, necessary contraction, they reduced staff and closed their manufacturing operation. Today, Tracy Porter is becoming a major player in the housewares design field. Here is what she says about the first year:

For us, it seems that in the beginning we found ourselves reacting all the time. We were so busy trying to keep up that it was really challenging to step outside of how we were growing our business and remember to be proactive. In the flurry of your entrepreneurial journey it is important to remember that you need to have goals and take steps to move toward them. Otherwise, it's easy for your business to take on a life of its own—one that might not be what you really envision.

What to Expect

If you are used to working in an office environment, and you are going it alone, expect to experience a certain amount of loneliness. Having a partner can mitigate that feeling somewhat, and so can the support of a loving family, but there's no denying that striking out on your own can be both lonely and frightening.

Expect to do a lot of grunt work. In all likelihood, you'll be the one to pick up the slack when everyone else has gone home (if there is anyone else). Expect to wrap packages, take out the trash, and do the cleaning up.

Expect to use up every favor you were ever owed. (You can't store favors in the favor bank forever, so you might as well withdraw them while they are still valid.) Get everyone you know to help out, scrub floors, paint shelves, spread the word, etc.

If you are hiring people, expect a certain amount of staff instability. Start-ups are inherently volatile, and employees can get skittish and jump to what they see as a surer thing. Try not to take these defections personally.

Expect to learn that running a business is nothing like what you thought it would be. Nothing but experience can prepare you for the realities, hidden costs, traumas, and highs of launching a business.

If you have been in or have run some other business before, expect to learn that certain lessons are transferable. Build on whatever knowledge you have about finance, marketing, and management.

Expect to find out that you like doing some things you never dreamed you'd like doing, and don't like doing things you thought you'd love. Maybe you'll find out you're a natural salesperson, manager, marketer, or numbers person.

Expect to expend more time, energy, and money than you thought you would have to. Several fold. Expect to find deep reservoirs of strength, stamina, and optimism within yourself. "The first year and a half," says Michele Rosier, of Flowers by Michele in Santa Monica, "I worked twenty-hour days, seven days a week. Expect the biggest stress you've ever had, and be prepared for the worst. If you're not passionate about it, you'll never make it."

Expect evolution and change. Be ready to react to new information about the marketplace and learn to anticipate it. Don't cling to an idea that is proving unworkable. If, however, you find that your product, or your store, is catching on, little by little, stick to your guns.

Expect not to make money for at least the first six months, maybe a year. Count yourself lucky if you don't lose money and downright blessed if you manage to eke out a small profit.

Expect a certain myopia to set in. You will begin to interpret everything in terms of how it will affect your business, including national elections, wars, famine, and weather conditions. Certain friends may begin to avoid you since you seem to want to discuss nothing else besides your business. You will be so busy, you'll hardly notice. If they are real friends, they'll still be there when things settle down a bit.

Expect to ride an emotional roller coaster. Leslie Ross, the founder of The Thymes Limited, the multimillion-dollar Minneapolis-based maker of bath, home-fragrance, and body-care products, still remembers the euphoria of her first "show" in which she introduced and sold many of the products she had been brewing up at home. Despite some early successes, Leslie was devastated when a manufacturer's rep she was courting rejected her. "I threw myself on the couch and cried," she said. Once she recovered, she picked herself up, brushed herself off, and went and hawked her products herself at local shopping centers.

Common Pitfalls in the First Year

Undercapitalization and cash-flow problems head this list. You should have cash reserves to carry you through at least the first six months, if not a year. If your overhead is very low, you may manage to eke out a profit before that. You may have heard the term "burn rate," which the high-flying Internet start-up world brought into the popular lexicon. Burn rate is simply the rate at which a business goes through its cash. Obviously, if the cash goes too fast, without any possibility of replenishment and without the business gaining any traction, you will quickly be out of business. To slow the burn rate, you may have to cut back on marketing, advertising, and staff, moves that may also inhibit growth.

Your cash needs will be higher the first year of business than in subsequent years, or at least less negotiable. Since you are new, unknown, and untested, suppliers will want you to pay up front. Only when you are established will they give you terms or credit. The first year is filled with relationship building, and in business, cash and delivering what you say you will go a long way on that score.

Try to anticipate cash needs as accurately as possible and have a plan in place, and a backup plan, for financing. Many entrepreneurs end up falling back on credit cards when things are tight, which is a ready but expensive source of cash. Easier said than done, it nonetheless is worth repeating that you should always try to secure money before desperation sets in and you really, really need it.

Managing Time and Stress

The first year of business, you are so green. Everyone wants an hour of your time, to tell you about their charity or their phone service. You learn how important it is to manage your time. I've come to realize that the twenty or thirty minutes of quiet time I have a day is very important."

—Paula Goldstein, Desana, Boston

I'm a big believer in the weekly checklist. You should use your brain for more creative things than remembering every tiny detail or chore that needs taking care of."

—Pam Scurry, Wicker Garden, New York

When it comes to managing time, some entrepreneurs are better than others. But no one can afford not to cultivate techniques to make sure that valuable time does not just slip away, and the things that truly need doing, get done. Excessively long and unproductive meetings, constant interruptions, including phone calls trying to sell you things you don't need, are all time-eaters. Develop a proactive strategy to deal with these situations early, such as limiting meetings and who attends them, controlling phone interruptions, with voice-mail or someone taking messages for you, and closing your door for blocks of time to dream, think, and follow through. If necessary, make appointments with yourself and make sure you keep them.

Set priorities. A good way to make sure you get something done that is difficult and anxiety-producing is to do it first thing in the morning when you are fresh. That way, you won't be worrying about it for the rest of the day. Try to complete deadline work early. At the end of every day, clean your desk, and organize yourself for the next day with a list of tasks, starting with the most dreaded one.

If you feel you are just going from crisis to crisis, or constantly in a reactive mode, as Tracy Porter did that first year, take a step back to assess where you are in relation to your goals and what steps you are taking to reach them. Are you making sure to leave time for things that might not seem as essential as putting out whatever fire has flared? Are you spending time on marketing? Are you networking? Are you planning?

For women with family commitments, it is also essential to build some flexibility into your schedule, to deal with the inevitable emergencies that arise.

Rhythms of Business

Our first year, the biggest surprise was December, the holiday season. We had no understanding of the siege that we would be under. In retail, you have to become really malleable, because there is no formula. It can be a glorious sunny Sunday and seventy-five degrees, and no one comes around. You can't be discouraged by fluctuations in day-to-day sales."

—Paula Goldstein, Desana, Boston

It would be nice if business always came in an even, steady, manageable flow. But this is seldom the case. When business is too meager, the problem is obvious. But too much business, more than you could have anticipated or planned for, can also put a major strain on you, your staff, and your resources. You may run out of stock or be overextended in terms of time and the ability to serve the clients you have. Hiring in a hurry can lead to hiring mistakes and overhiring.

Predicting sales volume is obviously not a science. Use the experience of the first year to gather a wealth of data about when you might expect droughts and floods of business activity. Take note of all the rhythms and use it for your planning in subsequent years. As time goes by, you may think you have a handle on this, but there will always be more surprises. The best way to prepare for the ebbs and flows of business is to have a plan in place to handle both the best- and the worst-case scenarios. What if your business suddenly takes off? How will you handle the volume? What if times are slow? Can you still pay your expenses and tide the business over?

When the going gets tough, as it inevitably will in the first year and probably in subsequent years, remind yourself of why you are doing this.

Hold on to your dreams and remember this is your passion. But also remember that although your business is an expression of you, it is *not* you. Even if the business dies, you will not.

Managing Windfalls

Windfalls can be pleasant surprises, but if you are not prepared for them, they can overwhelm you. Some entrepreneurs who have been featured in *Victoria* magazine have been so inundated with customers, requests for information, and orders that what seemed like a lucky, and deserved, break, actually turned into a major ordeal.

Debby DuBay of Limoges Antiques in Andover, Massacusetts, thought she had done a good job of anticipating response when *Victoria* first featured her shop in 1997. "I knew I would need a catalogue, so I had a professional one completed that pictured items for sale and their prices." She also had postcards of her shop and a picture business card printed. The flood of calls that resulted from the article, however, so surprised her that she quickly realized she had not budgeted for the expense of mailing a catalogue to everyone who called. She also realized that since her business was in one-of-a-kind antiques, a catalogue did not really work, since items once sold were no longer available. "I was overwhelmed for a year with requests for sold pieces," she says. But the experience taught her valuable lessons.

1. That a catalogue is not the way to go for a business dealing in one-of-a-kind pieces. (A web site is better, since it can be frequently updated.)

2. If you do have a catalogue, request a postage-paid envelope or charge a fee that will count toward the first order.

3. DuBay came up with a small, relatively inexpensive product to offer callers, a Limoges holiday ornament. "My product had to represent my shop perfectly," she says. "And that is what these beautiful ornaments did." The next time *Victoria* featured DuBay, in 1999, she was prepared.

Sylvia and Bill Varney's Fredericksburg Herb Farm were deluged with orders for an edible flower vinegar they entered in a competition sponsored by the National Association for the Specialty Food Trade. Their product won, and they discovered they could not fulfill all the wholesale orders that resulted. The windfall forced them to expand quickly, buying more land, and going from fifteen to twenty-seven employees.

If you know that you are going to be featured in a national magazine, especially one like *Victoria*, whose readers use the magazine as a buying guide, or even a local publication, and can reasonably expect a spike in business, start laying the groundwork to increase production if you need to. Beef up your web site and your printed collateral like brochures and catalogue. Get ready.

Building a Business for the Long Haul

You don't get a second chance to make a first impression, the old adage goes, and this is certainly true in business. While you are building your business, you are also building the public perception of your business, and if you get off on the wrong foot in this department, it will be difficult and time-consuming to undo the damage. Assume that you will be around for a long time. And assume that people will remember everything you ever did.

Your image is the sum total of your customers' impression of you. Everything contributes to it: your logo, your web site, your packaging, your business card, the look of your store, its location, how the phone is answered, and how the people who deal with the customers dress. Don't leave any detail unexamined.

Business has its own golden rule: Treat customers as you would want to be treated. Don't do just anything for a sale. Don't squeeze every last dollar out of a sale. Don't treat someone, whether a supplier or a customer, badly, especially when you plan to build a long-term relationship with them.

> *When you are building a business, you have to take a long-term view. Don't just do everything that's most expedient.*
>
> —Camilla Bergeron, antiques and estate jewelry dealer, New York

Make it a point to build up as wide a base of customers as possible. Overreliance on a single big customer is one of the most common causes of business failure. If that customer pulls out for any reason, your business is sunk. If you expand your staff and overhead because you have landed one big customer, you will end up holding the bag if that customer, for whatever reason, moves on.

If you are in manufacturing or wholesaling, you must expend extra effort and expense just to get your product out there and into the hands of the people who can influence others to buy it. This might mean sending free samples, if your product lends itself to that, and possibly going on the road yourself and taking it around.

As you build your business, you also need to build your brand. Your brand is your logo and your name, but it also the expectation of who you are, what you do, and how well you do it.

Growing

It is impossible to run a thriving business without changing and adapting to the ever-changing conditions of the market. Although growing entails a certain amount of risk, so, sometimes, does standing still. Because trends and the marketplace are inherently dynamic, if you stay in business for many years, chances are that yours will not be the same business it was when you first started out. Markets, technologies, and times change, and you will need to adapt, to recognize and seize new opportunities, to capitalize on customer appetites. No business can afford to stand still or to merely rest on its laurels.

Twenty-seven years ago Mary Ella Gabler started Peacock Alley, a business idea that stemmed from a pillow given to friends for Christmas presents, and which grew into a collection sold through Neiman Marcus and then expanded into a line of bedding products and ultimately into the retail, manufacturing, and wholesale operation it is today. "One thing is for sure," she says. "What you set out to do is not what it ends up being."

> *It's either grow or die.*
>
> —Gail Pittman, dinnerware designer

Sylvia Varney, of Fredericksburg Herb Farm, says that growth and evolution have been a necessity in her and husband Bill's multifaceted business. What started as a retail operation branched out into one involving manufacturing the herbal products sold in the shop, a spa, and more. "Customers come back and they want to know what's new," says Sylvia. "You can't keep still; people will demand that you grow."

If you have successfully carved out a niche, chances are that competitors will notice your success and make every effort to join you there, maybe even crowd you out. Staying one step ahead of copycats is just one reason to keep moving. One way to help you decide whether to grow or change your business is to ask yourself, what would happen if you made the change, or, more to the point, what will happen if you don't. Sometimes, it's riskier to stand still.

That said, you need to find a growth rate that is both comfortable for you and natural for your business. Runaway growth is not necessarily healthy. Some are more prepared for expansion than others, and not being prepared for it can lead to precipitous, even dooming mistakes.

AN ENTREPRENEUR VERSUS A SMALL-BUSINESS PERSON

There are those who want to run a small successful business based on something that they love doing, for whom success is simply being the master of their own ship, paying their own bills, and making a small profit. There is nothing wrong with that. Even remaining small can entail a great deal of adapting and changing as the marketplace evolves.

Debby DuBay, of Limoges Antiques in Andover, Massachusetts, deliberately opted to keep her business small, even though she had grown successful enough to expand it. After twenty years in the Air Force, she was looking for a tranquil low-stress life. But staying small should not be confused with standing still; it's more akin to running in place. DuBay has shown a canny ability of adapting to the market, capitalizing early on the web, and garnering a good deal of publicity for her small shop. In short, even a small-business person needs to be a little bit entrepreneurial, and some may be surprised by just how strongly an entrepreneurial a vein runs through them.

In growing a business, you always have to jump off cliffs. You're never not taking risks.

—Leeda MArting, Charleston Gardens

True entrepreneurs look at their businesses as a financial investment, not just as an expression of themselves. It is not merely a question of growing profits and their income, but growing the net worth of the company, which is how wealth is really built.

Leeda Marting, owner of Charleston Gardens, puts herself in this category. "My passion is business itself," she says. "An entrepreneur wants to grow something. A small-business person wants to stick with something small."

Ready for Expansion

DAWN HOUSER, graphic designer

A gifted and whimsical graphic designer, Dawn Houser went into business for herself shortly after she learned she was pregnant for the third time. She was torn between the call of motherhood and the need to spread her professional wings. "My priority was to be home with the kids," she says. "But I knew in my heart that I could not put off my career any longer."

To keep the balance in her life, she started slowly, approaching a rubber-stamp company that had shown interest in her work and gaining her first client. When she landed the prestigious stationery company Crane & Company as an account, she was really on her way. She now designs several collections for Crane. "It has been a slow process of building clients and keeping them happy," she says. "My job is done when the client looks at the finished product and says, 'This is *exactly* what I had envisioned!' or 'This logo (or calling card) is *me*. You have captured who I am!'"

Dawn started small and built her business without incurring much risk, a strategy she realizes perfectly suited her temperament and lifestyle. She worked from home, at unusual hours to avoid having to hire baby-sitters. Her goal was to have no overhead, to bill expenses directly to clients, and to earn a profit, however meager, right from the start. "Some women are risk takers and feel comfortable with that," she says. "Some are not. If I had taken risks, I probably would have had a nervous breakdown from the worry."

Once her daughter entered kindergarten, Dawn knew she was ready to expand her business. But she still wanted to do it in such a way that she would be available to plan and execute her children's birthday parties, help them with homework, and participate in the myriad other pleasures and demands of mothering. As a designer, she figured her options were either manufacturing her designs or licensing them out to other manufacturers. She quickly figured out that manufacturing was not for her and began to seek out licensing partners, a relationship in which a company purchases the rights to use your design on a particular product that they make. Not long after reaching that decision, she licensed with a tableware and gift-bags company. "Remember that adage, three or more of something makes a collection," she says. "In my mind, when I have five licensors, I will be legit."

With a clever web site, which includes a call to licensors, and an increasingly impressive list of clients, she is well on her way.

❖ GROWING IN A WAY THAT'S TRUE TO YOU

THE FACE STOCKHOLM STORY

The innovative makeup company from Sweden was catching on fast in the states by the mid-1990s, and Martina Arfwidson, the daughter of the mother-daughter team that owned it, was being swept along on a rising tide of success.

Barney's had insisted they open a FACE Stockholm boutique inside the department store, requiring that Arfwidson get a quick lesson in running a wholesale business as well as retail storefronts. In fact, Arfwidson, a trained singer, had not even planned a career in her mother's business. "I was just going to make enough to pay my rent and go have my singing career."

> *The proper way to grow is by releasing growth. The worst way is to push growth.*
>
> —Paul Hawken, *Growing a Business*

But the business was a whirlwind of activity and expansion, and after her singing group broke up, it became her sole focus. Though it was very successful, FACE Stockholm also made a number of missteps. "We opened spas and realized that doesn't work for us," Arfwidson says. "Hair salons don't work for us, either. We ended up closing a lot of locations." Still, the business grew, and by the late 1990s, venture capitalists were looking to fund the company's opening in hundreds of malls across the country. That's when the revelation came. "Mom and I were about to launch in some Marshall Fields store," Arfwidson recounts, "and we woke up in the middle of the night in the hotel and realized that we did not want to live like this. We decided to pull out of all department stores and not be in any malls. We wanted to have Billie Holiday tapes playing in our stores and for our salespeople to be able to show customers how a shade of lipstick looks in real sunlight."

Their move ruffled some feathers, but Arfwidson says they have never regretted it, and the business is still thriving. "For me the hardest lesson to learn was to say 'no.' We've realized that we are in charge, and we have to keep the big picture in mind. There's a part of me that resists becoming a big huge chain. I hope that shows in the shops." For Arfwidson, keeping the big picture in mind and keeping her sanity also meant moving the corporate offices out of Manhattan to a town on the Hudson two hours north, where she still presides over an empire, but at least gets to gaze out at nature and retreat to a beautiful old farmhouse nearby where she lives.

CONSULTING THE EXPERTS

Karen Krasne, owner of Extaordinary Desserts in San Diego, had dutifully and slowly grown her business carefully for a number of years. She started with used kitchen equipment and a limited menu of scrumptious desserts that she served with coffee or tea, then added tables, retail items from far-flung trips, muffins, and bagels as customer demand dictated, always careful to stay within budget.

Twelve years into her business, and with a lot of rough road behind her, she decided she wanted to take her business to the next level, explore other revenue streams, and restore some balance in her life. To help guide her in this change, she hired a management consultant in San Francisco who would examine her entire business and recommend a route. Among the strategies she is pursuing as a result are writing a book and developing a line of jams, jellies, and chutneys to be marketed wholesale and on a web site. When they are done, she'll hire a press agent to help get the word out. She's looking to hire more upper management to relieve her of some of the day-to-day burdens of running the cafe and create an incentive plan for employees. The management consultant also suggested she write a mission statement. "It's exciting to write a statement about who you are and how you can make a difference in the world," she says.

Expanding your business into new areas, or changing its course bares some resemblance to starting out. Consult the people you have relied on before to advise you, whether they are mentors, friends, business counselors, or other advisers. If you find you have outgrown the expertise of your usual advisers, seek out others. Consider hiring a management consultant to explore overlooked avenues, advise you on timing, costs, and the feasibility of doing what you want to do.

Be sure also to work with your accountant to help you set up a book-keeping structure for the expanded company, a tax-planning strategy, and a payroll system. If you are entering new legal areas, such as licensing, consult with your attorney. Don't go it alone. And get the advice you need.

HIRING MANAGEMENT CONSULTANTS

It can be beneficial to get professional advice on running or expanding your company, especially when you want to take it in a direction that may be new to you. Management consultants should provide expertise that your business does not already have. If you already have a solid strategy, it's a waste of time and money to hire someone just to rubber-stamp it. Generally, management consultants charge from $1,000 to $3,000 per day for their services, plus expenses. (If you can hire someone local, that will reduce expenses.) So, before you hire one, you should be very clear about what you want and need to accomplish.

The quality of management consultants varies widely, since they are not licensed. Anyone can call himself a management consultant. Make sure you check references and ask plenty of questions when you meet.

- Ask for examples of work they have done with other clients, the challenges, and the results. (Some of this information may be confidential, but they should be able to demonstrate their track record.) They should have experience with firms your company's size and in your industry, but not clients who are direct competitors, since that could be a conflict of interest.

- Make sure the consultant understands your business's particular needs and that the project being proposed is tailored to you. Consultants should be passionate about their work, but if they talk more about themselves, that could be a problem.

- Get clear on the time frame, when you can expect the proposal, and how much it will cost. You don't want any surprises when the bill comes.

- Find out who you will be working with. It may be that the person you meet with is not the one who will be working on the project.

COMMUNICATING WITH STAFF

When you are making changes and expanding your business, be sure to communicate what you are doing and why to your staff, since expansion will certainly effect their lives. Even the lowliest employee has a stake in the direction the company is taking. You need also to consider whether your existing staff can handle the expanded operation, or if you will be overwhelming their coping abilities. Honest, genuine communication works best. Give it and expect it back from your staff.

Your Changing Role in an Expanded Business

In an expanded business, your role will change. You may have to hire upper-level managers, like Krasne. You may have to hire other designers. If you are opening a second store, you will need someone to manage it. You will have to let go and delegate and be open to new ways of doing things. You will have to let other people do what they were hired to do. "A shortcoming of the entrepreneur is the belief that we can do it better than anyone else," says Helen Cox of As You like It Silver Shop, who confesses that she herself has suffered from this form of entrepreneuritis. "This thinking limits expansion of the business. We do not want to relinquish power to others."

If you are primarily a creative person, chances are that the business of taking care of business will take you away from some of the creative work. The business designer Rachel Ashwell started, Shabby Chic, grew into a multimillion-dollar empire from a relatively simple idea: stylish oversized furniture covered with washable white slipcovers. The growth has forced Ashwell to let go of the total design control she enjoyed when her company was much smaller, and that has not been an easy adjustment, she says. She calls being a creative person and running a company, a "hard marriage," one that she has had to work on every step of the way.

But she advises making time to keep in touch with the creative fire that once fueled your vision. For her, it means still spending time occasionally wandering through flea markets. For designer Claire Murray, it means continuing to base her company not far from the Nantucket landscape that inspired some of her first and most enduring rug designs.

THE DOWNSIDE OF EXPANSION

Growth and expansion are not always good or desirable. In fact, uncontrolled growth is one of the major reasons for business failure. Slow, steady, and incremental growth is much better. Growth and expansion require careful planning. Where is the money to pay for the additional inventory? Will the existing staff be able to handle the burgeoning workload or do you need to hire more people? Is hiring more staff the best solution or should you outsource certain functions? What happens if there is a recession, war, or some other event that drastically reduces consumer demand for your product?

THINGS TO CONSIDER BEFORE YOU EXPAND

- Are there economies of scale that will benefit an expanded operation?
- Are your competitors expanding?
- Can you finance the expansion internally?
- Will your customers tolerate your growing pains?
- Are you willing to play a less hands-on role in an expanded operation?
- By expanding, are you diluting beyond recognition the passion that originally inspired your business?

Expansion does not always mean more profit. You may be doing more volume by adding a second or third store and working harder, but, with all the additional overhead, not making any more money.

Lastly, expansion that carries you far away from your original vision or even passion, may make you richer, but less happy.

Making Mistakes

There has never been a successful entrepreneur who has not made mistakes. Most view making mistakes as an intrinsic, if sometimes painful, part of the process. Catching mistakes early, limiting the damage they do, and correcting and learning from them are what set the successful entrepreneurs apart. That and taking responsibility for, admitting to, and laughing about them. At the same time, once you realize that mistakes are and potentially costly, you will probably take steps to avoid them.

"We have certainly made our fair share of mistakes," says designer Tracy Porter. "We try to walk before we run whenever we are exploring a new opportunity and we always reserve the right to change our minds no matter how far in the exploration process we have gone. For me, there is comfort in knowing that it's never too late to change a direction especially if it is going to affect our lives. We try to be good self-evaluators in our business and in our personal lives, and if we see other companies making mistakes, we turn those situations on ourselves and ask if we are making the same choices."

Maintaining Balance

Life is more than an entrepreneurial adventure, and sooner or later we all realize we need to maintain balance in our lives and make sure we are attending to all of life's vital components: health, family, financial security, intellectual development, friendships, and professional and spiritual growth. Tending to these important areas of life is not only good for you, it will make you a better businessperson.

> I think an important lesson is keeping your ego in check, in life and in business. We're never going to have everything perfectly figured out, so why pretend that you do? I love the fact that we are learning about our business every day. Our company is just like our lives; it is constantly changing and evolving and with it we are growing too, and thank goodness for that. The learning part is what keeps it challenging and intriguing.

> We've learned so many lessons along the way and we have to constantly remind ourselves of what we have learned. Give yourself credit. In the beginning of anything, it's easy not to trust yourself, to think that everyone else must know so much more than you do. Surround yourself with people who have positive attitudes. You won't believe how much of a difference it will make on your most challenging days. Be true to yourself and keep an open mind.

> —Tracy Porter, designer, Princeton, Wisconsin

Appendix I

Dawn Houser, a mother of three from San Antonio, Texas, provides graphic design services for a variety of clients. Here is a template of her standard agreement, or contract, and her explanations of each item.

Date:

To: [Client name]
[Address]

Order Confirmation:
[This is where you state exactly what you are selling and exactly what the client is buying.]

Fee Summary:
[This is where you break down the fees.]

Terms:

1. *Time for payment.* Payment is due within thirty (30) days of receipt of invoice. A 1.5-percent monthly service charge will be billed for late payment. Any advances or partial payments shall be indicated under Fee Summary above.

2. *Default in payment.* The Client shall assume responsibility for all collection of legal fees necessitated by default in payment.

3. *Grant of rights.* The grant of reproduction rights is conditioned on receipt of payment.

4. *Reimbursable expenses.* Costs directly associated with the design and production of the work outlined in this agreement are reimbursable expenses. These expenses shall include, but are not limited to, artwork materials, photocopies, fax and long distance charges, postage, Federal Express, shipping, and any travel expenses. Receipts will be obtained and submitted with the invoice.

5. *Sales tax.* The Client shall be responsible for the payment of sales tax, if any such tax is due.

6. *Cancellation.* In the event of cancellation or breach by the Client, the Artist shall retain ownership of all rights of copyright and the original artwork, including sketches and any other preliminary materials. The Client shall pay the artist according to the following schedule: 50 percent of original fee if cancelled after preliminary sketches are completed, 100 percent if cancelled after completion of finished art.

7. *Revisions.* This contract covers only the services outlined. Changes in the scope of work, revisions of approved final design, or additions to the original assignment may result in additional creative fees and/or production expenses. Revisions not due to the fault of the Artist shall be billed separately.

8. *Credit lines.* On any contributions for magazine or book use, the Artist shall receive name credit in print.

9. *Unauthorized use.* Client will indemnify Artist against all claims and expenses, including reasonable attorney's fees, arising from uses for which no release was requested in writing or uses exceeding the authority granted by a release.

10. *Arbitration.* Any disputes in excess of $3,000 arising out of this Agreement shall be submitted to binding arbitration before the Joint Ethics Committee or a mutually agreed-upon arbitrator pursuant to the rules of the American Arbitration Association. The Arbitrator's award shall be final, and judgment may be entered in any court having jurisdiction thereof. The Client shall pay all arbitration and court costs, reasonable attorney's fees, and legal interest on any award of judgment in favor of the Artist.

11. *Acceptance of terms.* The signature of both parties shall evidence acceptance of terms.

Consented and agreed to

Date

Dawn Houser, Artist   Client

Appendix 2

FOR IMMEDIATE RELEASE

CONTACT: Shirley Wolf
Director of Public Relations
802-674-6017 x240

CLAIRE MURRAY® SUMMER/FALL DESIGNS
REFLECT HER NANTUCKET ROOTS

ASCUTNEY, VT (April, 2001) – World-renowned textile designer, Claire Murray introduces her new collection of 100-percent wool, hand-hooked rugs reflecting a "return to her Nantucket roots". Claire is well known for being inspired by the natural beauty and coastal treasures of Cape Cod and the Islands, her new Coastal collection takes us back to Nantucket, where it all began.

Claire Murray's signature palette of soft periwinkle, delicate corals, vibrant garden greens and Nantucket-sky blues are reflected in her charming shoreline village scenes, coastal garden motifs and new Nautical collection. The new Coastal collection of 2' x 3' area rugs include By The Sea Small, By The Sea Cottage, Coastal Fisherman Small and Coastal Village Small. Her Nautical Collection in a variety of sizes, features classic ocean icons such as lighthouses, compasses and flags in vibrant colors that all "sea captains" will hold dear.

Complimenting this Nantucket-inspired collection are Claire's new Garden designs abounding with the flowers she loves. "The colors of flowers are more vibrant by the sea," reflects Ms. Murray, who is also known for her award-winning gardens on Cape Cod. Garden Lattice is a delightful 3' round with a unique scalloped edge in both a black or ivory background. Also in the collection are a series of Botanical additions bringing the pleasures of Claire's garden into your home. The new Claire's Garden rugs reflect a soft, sophisticated look in both large and small sizes. They have been most enthusiastically received!

Back to her Nantucket roots... It's not only where Claire Murray learned the traditional art of rug hooking, it's where a hobby and passion became an internationally famous business. Claire Murray's unprecedented style which combines the look of contemporary Americana with her rich colors and beautiful motifs have brought this historic handicraft in step with today's designing trends.

In addition to introducing beautiful new rug designs, Claire Murray has expanded her already-extensive licensed product lines to include a sleep and loungewear line, a new collection of bath and kitchen accessories as well as a new, high-end bedding line complete with coordinating hand-hooked wool rugs.

Claire Murray has not only changed the way we look at our floors;
she is changing the way we look at our entire homes.

Appendix 3

BUSINESS IS BLOOMING

Exclusive Aura of Herbal Products Flourish for Texas Couple

(Date—Frederickburg, Texas) Fredericksburg Herb Farm is a little 15-year-old company that grows, makes, and sells sought-after herbs, gourmet foods, skin care, and aromatherapy products. Many others do one or some of the same thing, but owners Bill and Sylvia Varney have an approach to the business that can only be called one of passion.

The expert couple keep no secrets. They have authored *Herbs: Growing and Using Plants of Romance,* a 1999 Benjamin Franklin Award winner for agriculture and gardening ($18.95; Ironwood Press), *Along the Garden Path*, a cookbook ($24.95; Favorite Recipes Press), and write a quarterly *Farm Friendly Newsletter* ($2; www.fredericksburgherbfarm.com).

The Varneys garden for function and fun, and encourage gardeners and gardener wannabes to do so too. "Herbs beg to be touched, smelled, nibbled, worn," says Sylvia Varney. "Whether people visit our farm, or our web site, I want the experience to be sensory therapeutic."

Each of their farm's six herb gardens used for producing their products is planted around a theme. Granite markers, serious and whimsical, are sited to explain and inspire. What's seen in the garden is usually in pots for sale.

They package with an environmentally friendly simplicity and label with an almost more-than-you-need-to-know green-thumb text.

They operate two retail shops at the 14.5-acre farm, one on Main Street in Fredericksburg. Texas. They also own an organic restaurant; a day spa offering herbal wraps, massages, facials; and a bed and breakfast for customers wanting an experience of "herbal immersion." Products are available at www.fredericksburgherbfarm.com, by mail-order catalogue and wholesale.

They urge employees to get plant-smart and cultivate their own garden too in order to better answer customer questions.

The Varneys have developed a following that has other natural product purveyors, wholesale, and Internet companies green with envy. Customers swear by Fredericksburg Herb Farm cosmetics, candles, and vinegars. Exclusive retailers like Neiman Marcus and SelfCare.com sell them. The beautiful and fashionable from around the world converge on the farm's store. Numerous investors have made offers to Bill and Sylvia to buy Fredericksburg Herb Farm.

Fredericksburg Herb Farm offers a powerful lesson in the cachet that can come from digging in the opposite direction of all the competition. "Our approach is a very hands-on one," says Bill Varney. "I encourage everyone to grow herbs themselves—most require so little care."

#

Contact:
Bill Varney, Fredericksburg Herb Farm, P.O. Drawer 927, Fredericksburg, TX 78624; (830) 997-8615; fax: (830) 997-5069; e-mail: Wvarney@fredericksburgherbfarm.com

Appendix 4

ROMANCE DESIGN ARTS, INC.
BALANCE SHEET
DECEMBER 31, 2000

ASSETS

Current assets	
Cash	$18,403
Accounts receivable, net of all allowance for bad debts	23,479
Inventory	12,766
Prepaid expenses	2,953
Total current assets	57,601
Fixed assets, net of accumulated depreciation of $18,335	25,503
Organizational costs, net of accumulated amortization of $365	435
Security deposits	1,400
Total assets	$ 84,939

LIABILITIES AND STOCKHOLDERS' EQUITY

Current liabilities	
Accounts payable	$2,063
Notes payable—short term	6,345
Sales tax payable	1,455
Payroll tax payable	1,738
Corporate income tax payable	5,247
Total current liabilities	16,848
Notes payable—long term	13,327
Total liabilities	30,175
Stockholders' equity	
Common stock	10,000
Retained earnings	44,764
Total stockholders' equity	54,764
Total Liabilities and Stockholders' Equity	$84,939

See Accountants' Compilation Report

Appendix 5

ANNUAL INCOME, OR P&L, STATEMENT FOR FICTIONAL DESIGN SERVICES COMPANY:

ROMANCE DESIGN ARTS, INC.
BALANCE SHEET
YEAR ENDED DECEMBER 31, 1999

Revenue	$183,370
Cost of goods sold	56,104
Gross profit	127,366
Payroll expense	30,875
Payroll taxes	4,546
Employee benefits	4,795
Selling expense	4,855
Auto expense	6,104
Travel expense	3,955
Meals and entertainment expense	3,314
Promotion expense	1,015
Rent	12,723
Telephone	5,880
Office expense	2,310
Dues and subscriptions	878
Insurance	3,307
Utilities	1,149
Postage and delivery	1,501
Professional fees	2,930
Interest expense	1,509
Depreciation expense	1,192
Total expenses	92,838
Net income before provision for income taxes	34,428
Provision for income taxes	8,200
Net income	26,228
Retained earnings—beginning	18,536
Retained earnings—ending	$ 44,764

See Accountants' Compilation Report

Note: The sample balance sheet and income statement were prepared by Steven M. DelSanto, CPA, partner in the firm of DelSanto and DeFreitas, CPAs, 14 Vervalen Street, Closter, New Jersey 07624.

Appendix 6

XYZ Corporation, Inc.
EMPLOYEE HANDBOOK

This employee handbook has been prepared for your information and understanding of the policies, philosophies, and practices and benefits of XYZ Corporation. PLEASE READ IT CAREFULLY. Upon completion of your review of this handbook, please sign the statement below and return it to your personnel representative by the due date. A reproduction of this acknowledgment appears at the back of this booklet for your records.

I, _____, have received and read a copy of the XYZ Corporation (The Company) Employee Handbook, which outlines the goals, policies, benefits and expectations of The Company, as well as my responsibilities as an employee.

I have familiarized myself, at least generally, with the contents of this handbook. By my signature below, I acknowledge, understand, accept, and agree to comply with the information contained in the Employee Handbook provided to me by The Company. I understand this handbook is not intended to cover every situation that may arise during my employment, but is simply a general guide to the goals, policies, practices, benefits, and expectations of The Company.

I understand that The Company Employee Handbook is not a contract of employment and should not be deemed as such, and that I am an employee at will.

(Employee signature)

Please return by: _____
(put date here)

Note: This sample acknowledgement form is from Onlinewbc.org, the web site operated by the Small Business Administration, specifically geared to women entrepreneurs. The URL for this document is: http://www.onlinewbc.org/DOCS/manage/hrpol_ak.html.

Resources

FINANCING

Count Me In for Women's Economic Independence—online, microlender for women; loans of $500 to $10,000. www.count-me-in.org/.

Women's Growth Capital Fund—makes equity investments in start-up or expanding women-owned businesses. Canal Square, 1054 31st Street NW, Suite 110, Washington, DC 20007; (202) 342-1431; e-mail: info@wgcf.com.

Colorado Business Bank, 821 17th Street, Denver, CO 80202; (303) 293-2265. Founded as The Women's Bank in 1977, the name has changed but the bank is still known to be attuned to the needs of women business owners.

BOOKS

201 Ideas for Your Small Business, by Jane Applegate (Bloomberg Small Business)

Guerrilla Financing: Alternate Techniques to Finance Any Small Business, by Bruce Blechman and Jay Conrad Levinson (Houghton Mifflin)

Business Capital for Women, by Emily Card and Adam Miller (MacMillan)

Growing a Business, by Paul Hawken (Fireside)

How to Write a Winning Business Plan, by Joseph Mancuso (Simon & Schuster)

How to Write a Business Plan, by Mike McKeever (Nolo Press)

How Much Should I Charge? Pricing Basics for Making Money Doing What You Love, by Ellen Rohr. (Maxrohr, 1999.) Order by phone: 877MAXROHR, or online: www.barebonesbiz.com.

Where Did the Money Go? Easy Accounting Basics for the Business Owner Who Hates Numbers, by Ellen Rohr. (Maxrohr, 1999.) Order by phone: 877MAXROHR, or online: www.barebonesbiz.com.

The Ernst & Young Business Plan Guide, by Eric Siegel, Brian R. Ford, Jay M. Bornstein (John Wiley & Sons). Includes templates of financial instruments like balance sheets, profit-and-loss statement, cash-flow statements.

301 Do-It-Yourself Marketing Ideas, by the Editors of *Inc.* magazine (Inc. Publishing).

"Understanding Cash Flow: Sound Cash Management and Borrowing," pamphlet available from your local Small Business Administration chapter or by calling (800) 827-5722.

Business Plan Handbook (Rector Press). Contains examples of real business plans.

WEB SITES

www.americanexpress.com/smallbusiness/resources—American Express's web site for entrepreneurs.

www.bcentral.com—information on how to develop a business plan and raise capital.

www.bplans.com—sample plans, start up calculations, financing information.

www.eeoc.gov—the U.S. Equal Employment Opportunity Commission web site for information on what constitutes discrimination in hiring and firing.

www.freemerchant.com—template-driven program to set up simple online stores for do-it-yourselfers.

www.free-publicity.com—offers examples of press releases as well as press release writing services.

www.inc.com—Inc. magazine's site filled with articles and advice for small-business owners and entrepreneurs just starting out.

www.marketingangel.com—includes sample press releases and good marketing and PR advice for entrepreneurs.

www.onlinewbc.org—practical information geared to women entrepreneurs; tutorials, downloadable forms, basic accounting, inspiration, and practical advice.

www.sba.gov/ADVO/stats—helps you find a bank friendly to small-business borrowers; organized by state so you can find a bank in your area.

www.SBTV.com—Small Business Television online network—advice, dialogue, articles.

www.startupbiz.com—advice, resources, expert referrals; downloadable legal, investment, web site, marketing and human resources templates.

www.usdoj.gov/crt/ada/adahom1.html—home page of the Americans with Disabilities Act, for more information on job discrimination.

www.uspto.gov—The U.S. Patent and Trademark Office

www.victoriamag.com—Click on Entrepreneur Workshop. Lots of concrete tools, networking possibilities, and inspirational stories. Downloadable template and forms for business plans, income statements, etc.

www.womenswire.com/smallbiz/bizbox/finance.html—sample spreadsheets, boilerplate human resources forms, balance sheet templates, cash-flow budget worksheets, income statement templates, and more.

BUSINESS PLAN SOFTWARE

Plan a Business Plan—provides a prewritten 90-page business plan you can customize. (800) 644-4892. $69.95.

Plan Write for Business 5.0—provides a questionnaire on details of business and financial projections which you fill out. It then creates documents including cash-flow statements and charts demonstrating the strengths of your business idea.

Small Business Administration's business plan software—contact the SBA at (800) 827-5722, or visit their web site at www.sba.gov.

ORGANIZATIONS

National Association of Women Business Owners (NAWBO)—nationwide membership organization with regional chapters. National Headquarters, 1411 K Street NW, Suite 1300, Washington, DC 20005; (202) 347-8686, (800) 556-2926; e-mail: national@nawbo.org.

Small Business Administration
(800) 827-5722; www.sba.gov.

Service Corps of Retired Executives (SCORE), 409 Third Street, S.W., 6th Floor, Washington, D.C. 20024; (800) 634-0245; www.score.org.

Small Business Development Centers
These are usually, but not always, located at your local university.

Small Business in Canada

One-third of all Canadian firms are owned by women, and these woman-owned firms provide more jobs that the Canadian Business Top 100 Companies combined.

Canada Business Service Centers (CBSC)—The Canadian equivalent to the SBA is a network of centers throughout Canada offering support services for small businesses. Their web site, www.cbsc.org, offers online workshops; business plan guides; and listings of federal, provincial, and territorial programs and services.

Entrepreneurs and Businesses
Featured in *Turn Your Passion Into Profits*

AMES, JOYCE
Joyce Ames Lampshades
254 West 73rd Street
New York, NY 10023
(212) 799-8995
e-mail: joyceames7@aol.com
Custom-designed lampshades with
vintage fabrics, by appointment only

ANDERSON, MARY
Mary Nell's
270 Riverside Drive
New York, NY 10025
(212) 865-6010
Custom-designed decoupage plates

ARFWIDSON, MARTINA
FACE Stockholm
110 Prince Street
New York, NY 10012
(888) 334-3223
e-mail: contactus@facestockholm.com
www.facestockholm.com
Stores throughout U.S. and Europe
offer cosmetics, skincare and makeup
tools

BERGERON, CAMILLA
Camilla Dietz Bergeron
Antique Jewelry
818 Madison Avenue, 4th Floor
New York, NY 10021
(212) 794-9100
Antique and estate jewelry

COLE, REBECCA
Rebecca Cole Designs
41 King Street
New York, NY 10014
(212) 255-4797
e-mail: pottedgardens@aol.com
Floral and garden designer, television
personality

CONIGLIARO, CYNTHIA
Archivia
944 Madison Avenue
New York, NY 10021
(212) 439-9194
www.archivia.com
Store offering books on architecture,
gardens, decorative arts, interior
design

COX, HELEN
As You Like It Silver Shop
3033 Magazine Street
New Orleans, LA 70115
(800) 828-2311
e-mail: ayliss@bellsouth.net
www.asyoulikeitsilvershop.com
Vintage and heirloom silver shop

DARNI, ULLA
Ulla Darni Studios
Route 23, Box 65
Acra, NY 12405
(518) 622-3566
Handpainted glass lampshades

DIMMICK, CHRISTINE
Good Home Co.
(888) GHC-2862
www.goodhomeco.com
Manufacture and wholesale of home
and body-care items made with
natural ingredients

DUBAY, DEBBY
Limoges Antiques
20 Post Office Avenue
Andover, MA 01810
(978) 470-8773
www.limogesantiques.com
Store specializing in fine, handpainted
antique porcelain

FLAX, KATE
Kate's Paperie
8 West 13th Street
New York, NY 10011
(212) 633-0570
www.katespaperie.com
Fine paper and stationery supplies,
three stores in Manhattan

FORLEY, DIANE
Verbena
54 Irving Place
New York, NY 10003
(212) 260-5454
www.verbenarestaurant.com
Restaurant serving fresh, seasonal,
gourmet cuisine in a serene, upscale
environment

FOX, ANN
Room Service
4354 Lovers Lane
Dallas, TX 75225
(214) 369-7666
Store offering floral-themed home
furnishings, gifts and accessories

GABLER, MARY ELLA
Peacock Alley Linens
3210 Armstrong Avenue
Dallas, TX 75207
(214) 520-6736
(800) 652-3818

334 East 59th Street
New York, NY 10022
(212) 751-7005
(800) 496-2880
www.peacockalley.com
Purveyor of fine, classic, luxury
linens for bed and bath

GARRETON, ISABEL
Isabel Garreton, Inc.
4061 Miraleste Drive
Rancho Palos Verdes, CA 90275
(310) 833-7768
e-mail: igarreton@earthlink.net
www.isabelgarreton.com
Design and manufacture of
children's apparel

GOLDSTEIN, PAULA
Desana
211 Newbury Street
Boston, MA 02116
(617) 450-9599
(888) 5-DESANA
e-mail: desana211@aol.com
www.desana.com
Store offering custom-designed
fragrances and accessories

GOODRICH, JANE
Saturn Press Cards
P.O. Box 368
Swan's Island, ME 04685
Handpressed greeting cards

HOUSER, DAWN
Dawn Houser
418 Laramie Drive
San Antonio, TX 78209
(210) 930-0373
e-mail: howzr@aol.com
www.dawnhouser.com
Freelance product and licensing
design

KNIGHT, PAULETTE
The Ribbonerie
191 Potrero Avenue
San Francisco, CA 94103
(415) 626-6184
e-mail: theribbon@msn.com
www.theribbonerie.com
Specialty ribbons and notions shop

KRASNE, KAREN
Extraordinary Desserts
2929 Fifth Avenue
San Diego, CA 92103
(619) 294-7001
e-mail: xdesserts@aol.com
www.extraordinarydesserts.com
Gourmet dessert cafe offering unusual
housewares for sale

JONES, CHARMAINE
Isn't That Special Outrageous Cakes
720 Monroe Street
Hoboken, NJ 07030
(201) 216-0123
(212) 722-0678
e-mail: cakediva@aol.com
www.cakediva.com
Custom-designed cakes for weddings
and special occasions

JONES, MARGARET
Scriptura
5423 Magazine Street
New Orleans, LA 70115
(504) 897-1555
Fine-paper emporium

KERR, PAT
Pat Kerr Designs
200 Wagner Place
Memphis, TN 38103
(901) 525-LACE
Baby and bridal couture;
special events planning

MANCHESTER, MARSHA
Milady's Mercantile
No street address
(508) 946-2121
e-mail: Miladylinens@mediaone.net
Fine, vintage linens and laces for
collectors, by appointment only and
at specialty shows

MARTING, LEEDA
Charleston Gardens
61 Queen Street
Charleston, SC 29401
(800) 469-0118
(843) 723-0252
e-mail:
marting@charlestongardens.com
www.charlestongardens.com
Retail store and mail-order business
offering garden accessories

MURRAY, CLAIRE
Claire Murray Designs
P.O. Box 390
Ascutney, VT 05030
(Corporate Office)
(800) 252-4733
www.clairemurray.com
Retail, wholesale, design and licensing
business specializing in wool, hand-
hooked rugs

PITTMAN, GAIL
Gail Pittman, Inc.
P.O. Box 779
Ridgeland, MI 39158
(601) 856-5646
e-mail: info@gailpittman.com
www.gailpittman.com
Handpainted dinnerware and
accessories

PORTER, TRACY
Tracy Porter
544 West Water Street
Princeton, WI 54968
(888) 382-4500
(920) 295-4500
www.tracyporter.com
store@tracyporter.com
Whimsical, often floral-themed house-
ware design and licensing

POUILLON, NORA
Restaurant Nora
2132 Florida Avenue NW
Washington, DC 20008
(202) 462-5143
www.noras.com
Gourmet organic restaurant

ROSIER, MICHELE
Flowers by Michele at Fred Segal
500 Broadway
Santa Monica, CA 90401
(310) 656-0688
Custom-designed floral
arrangements

SCURRY, PAMELA
Wicker Garden's Children
Wicker Garden's Baby
1327 Madison Avenue
New York, NY 10128
(212) 410-7001
Store offering wicker and baby furni-
ture as well as baby clothes

SMITH-PETERSON, GAIL
Buckingham Mercantile
2189 San Elijo Avenue
Cardiff-by-the-Sea, CA 92007
(760) 436-7666
www.buckinghamgear.com
Store offering clothing for children,
babies and women, gifts and
accessories

VARNEY, SYLVIA
Fredericksburg Herb Farm
P.O. Drawer 927
Fredericksburg, TX 78624-0927
Main Office: (830) 997-8615
Orders Only: (800) 259-HERB
e-mail: herbfarm@ktc.com
www.fredericksburgherbfarm.com
Multifaceted business offering herbal
products, spa, and retail

WADE, LINDA
Putti
1104 Yonge Street
Toronto, Ontario, Canada M4W2L6
(416) 972-7652
putti@sympatico.ca
Store that sells antiques; cherubs often
featured

WASHINGTON, COOKIE
Phenomenal Women Designs
1943 Culver Avenue
Charleston, SC 29407
(843) 769-4927
e-mail: cookiesews@aol.com
Custom-designed wedding dresses